Read the Inside Story of Witchcraft

Witchcraft from the Inside presents an insider's look at the state of Witchcraft today and its impact on twentieth-century America. Originally published in 1971, this groundbreaking book reviews the attempted destruction of Witchcraft and other Pagan religions by the Christian Church in Europe and the growing Wican/Pagan trends in America at the time. In this updated edition, author Ray Buckland retains the historical synopsis of Witchcraft and includes documentation of the Salem Witch trials in New England. Using nonsexist language and a nondenominational approach, *Witchcraft from the Inside* raises issues of crucial concern to both Pagans and non-Pagans in America today. *Witchcraft from the Inside* explores teen Witchcraft, Dianic (feminist) Witchcraft, modern Wica (or "Wicca") and its rebirth in the 1950s, faeries, and other trends taking America into the twenty-first century.

About the Author

Ray Buckland has spent nearly half a century investigating various aspects of the occult and has been active in Wica, or modern-day white Witchcraft, for more than a quarter of a century. A protegé of the late Dr. Gerald Gardner, he was instrumental in introducing the Gardnerian branch of Wica to the United States in the early 1960s. In the early 1970s he founded the Seax-Wica branch of the Old Religion and has since seen it spread and prosper.

Ray has written a large number of books, many of them now regarded as classics in their field. He has appeared on both national and international television and radio, and has spent many years lecturing and holding seminars across the country.

To Write to the Author

If you wish to contact the author or would like more information about this book, please write to the author in care of Llewellyn Worldwide and we will forward your request. Both the author and publisher appreciate hearing from you and learning of your enjoyment of this book and how it has helped you. Llewellyn Worldwide cannot guarantee that every letter written to the author can be answered, but all will be forwarded. Please write to:

Ray Buckland
c/o Llewellyn Worldwide
P.O. Box 64383-K101, St. Paul, MN 55164-0383, U.S.A.

Please enclose a self-addressed, stamped envelope for reply, or $1.00 to cover costs.
If outside U.S.A., enclose international postal reply coupon.

Free Catalog from Llewellyn

For more than 90 years Llewellyn has brought its readers knowledge in the fields of metaphysics and human potential. Learn about the newest books in spiritual guidance, natural healing, astrology, occult philosophy and more. Enjoy book reviews, new age articles, a calendar of events, plus current advertised products and services. To get your free copy of *Llewellyn's New Worlds of Mind and Spirit*, send your name and address to:

Llewellyn's New Worlds of Mind and Spirit
P.O. Box 64383-K101, St. Paul, MN 55164-0383, U.S.A.

Llewellyn's World Religion and Magic Series

Witchcraft from the Inside

Origins of the Fastest Growing Religious Movement in America

Revised and Enlarged Third Edition

Raymond Buckland

1995
Llewellyn Publications
St. Paul, Minnesota 55164–0383, U.S.A.

THIRD EDITION
First Printing, 1995

Cover design by Katie Viren

Photographs and illustrations by Raymond Buckland
Editing, design, and layout by David Godwin

Library of Congress Cataloging in Publication Data
Buckland, Raymond.
    Witchcraft from the inside : origins of the fastest growing
religious movement in America / Raymond Buckland. — Rev. and enl.
3rd ed.
    p.   cm. — (Llewellyn's world religion and magic series)
    Includes bibliographical references and index.
    ISBN 1–56718–101–5 : $12.95
    1. Witchcraft.   2. Witchcraft—History.   I. Title.   II. Series:
Llewellyn's world religion and magic series.
BF1566.B77   1995
133.4'3—dc20   94–44804
                                                              CIP

Llewellyn Publications
A Division of Llewellyn Worldwide, Ltd.
P.O. Box 64383, St. Paul, MN 55164-0383

Llewellyn's World Religion and Magic Series

At the core of every religion, at the foundation of every culture, there is MAGICK.

Magick sees the world as alive, as the home which humanity shares with beings and powers both visible and invisible, with whom and which we can interface to either our advantage or disadvantage—depending upon our awareness and intention.

Religious worship and communion is one kind of magick, and just as there are many religions in the world, so are there many magickal systems.

Religion and magick are ways of seeing and relating to the creative powers, the living energies, the all-pervading spirit, the underlying intelligence that is the universe within which we and all else exist.

Neither religion nor magick conflict with science. All share the same goals and the same limitations: always seeking truth, forever haunted by human limitations in perceiving that truth. Magick is "technology" based upon experience and extrasensory insight, providing its practitioners with methods of greater influence and control over the world of the invisible before it impinges on the world of the visible.

The study of world magick not only enhances your understanding of the world in which you live, and hence your ability to live better, but brings you into touch with the inner essence of your long evolutionary heritage and most particularly—as in the case of the magickal system identified most closely with your genetic inheritance—with the archetypal images and forces most alive in your whole consciousness.

Other Books by Raymond Buckland

Anatomy of the Occult (Weiser, 1977)
Buckland's Complete Book of Witchcraft (Llewellyn, 1975, 1977, 1987)
Buckland's Gypsy Fortunetelling Deck (Llewellyn, 1989)
The Tree: Complete Book of Saxon Witchcraft (Weiser, 1974)
Doors to Other Worlds (Llewellyn, 1993)
Here Is the Occult (House of Collectibles, 1974)
The Magick of Chant-O-Matics (Parker, 1978)
A Pocket Guide to the Supernatural (Ace, 1969)
Practical Candleburning Rituals (Llewellyn, 1970, 1976, 1982)
Practical Color Magick (Llewellyn, 1983)
Scottish Witchcraft (Llewellyn, 1991)
Secrets of Gypsy Dream Reading (Llewellyn, 1990)
Secrets of Gypsy Fortunetelling (Llewellyn, 1988)
Secrets of Gypsy Love Magick (Llewellyn, 1990)
Witchcraft Ancient and Modern (HC, 1970)
Witchcraft...the Religion (Buckland Museum, 1966)

With Hereward Carrington
Amazing Secrets of the Psychic World (Parker, 1975)

With Kathleen Binger
The Book of African Divination (Inner Traditions, 1992)

Under the pseudonym "Tony Earll"
Mu Revealed (Warner Paperback Library, 1970)

Fiction
The Committee (Llewellyn, 1993)

Video
Witchcraft Yesterday and Today (Llewellyn, 1990)

Forthcoming
Ray Buckland's Magic Cauldron (Galde Press, 1995)
Truth About Spirit Communication (Llewellyn, 1995)
Advanced Candle Magick
Cardinal's Sin (fiction)

For Tara

and for Doreen Valiente, for all her work
in establishing the Wica we know today

Contents

Gerald Gardner in front of the Witches' Mill, Castletown, Isle of Man

FOREWORD

For about four hundred years Witchcraft, to all intents and purposes, has been dead, bludgeoned to death in the late Middle Ages. During and since that time there have been many hundreds, if not thousands, of books written on the subject of Witchcraft—almost all, perhaps not unnaturally, from the point of view of the Christian Church. However, with the new "Age of Enlightenment," with the "thinking people" of the twentieth century, a few books have finally appeared endeavoring to look at the subject from a less biased point of view. The trend was started by the late Dr. Margaret Murray and was quickly followed by other scholars...people with no particular axe to grind. What they found was enlightening. Witchcraft, they said, was not at all what we had been so sternly taught to believe it to be. It was not devil-worship and black magick but a benign, positive, nature-based religion.

Confirmation of these scholarly theories was not long in coming for, it seemed, Witchcraft had not died after all! It had lain hidden, feigning death, awaiting the chance to once more come out and practice openly and unafraid. With modern open-mindedness, together with the repeal of the last anti-Witchcraft Laws, it was free to do so.

At last, then, the explanation of what Witchcraft really was/is could be given. In England the late Dr. Gerald Brousseau Gardner was the first to speak out for the Witches (*Witchcraft Today*, Rider, 1954). As a High Priest himself he was able to tell as much as might be told to a non-initiate.

Gardner reluctantly saw "the Craft" as a dying religion—for religion is exactly what it is—on its last legs after being so long in seclusion. But more than forty years have now passed since Gardner first wrote and the scene has changed dramatically. Alongside the so-few surviving groups, or covens, known to Gardner have emerged many more throughout the whole of Europe and elsewhere. From the few known covens which Gardner himself founded, many hundreds have sprung, on both sides of the Atlantic and around the world. And other denominations, or traditions, of Witchcraft have come out of hiding so that today a would-be Witch has a wide selection from which to choose. "The Craft" has grown at an unprecedented rate. This is a very laudable state of affairs and one which would surely have cheered the heart of the late Dr. Gardner.

The first edition of this present book, *Witchcraft from the Inside*, appeared in 1971 and was written at that time because Gardner's books, and a few others that had followed them, had gone out of print. Again, the passage of time has changed that. Many of those important early books from the 1950s and 1960s have been reprinted and are once more available. Yet this present volume, newly updated and enlarged, is still valid, giving a view of Witchcraft in its formative years in the United States and looking further, at the state of the religion today.

After so many centuries of hearing only one side of the Witchcraft story, it is time to enlarge on the other.

—RAYMOND BUCKLAND

1994

1: Life Amongst Death

What is Witchcraft? What is a Witch? The popular conception of a Witch is that of commercial Halloween: a humpbacked old hag bent over a broomstick as she flies through the air on some nefarious errand. As Harsnet put it, writing in 1603:

> An old weather-beaten crone, having her chin and knees meeting for age, walking like a bow, leaning on a staff, hollow-eyed, untoothed, furrowed, having her limbs trembling with palsy, going mumbling through the streets.

She consorts with the Devil and spends her time blasting the poor farmers' crops and making their cows run dry of milk, we are told.

But how accurate is this picture? What happened to the earlier ideas? Circe, the famous Witch of the *Odyssey*, is described by Homer as a

> goddess with lovely hair…radiant…the
> beautiful goddess singing in a lovely voice…
> (in) a white shining robe, delicate and lovely,
> with a fine girdle of gold about her waist.

Medea, the Witch in the Golden Fleece adventures, is a beautiful young princess of whom Jason said:

> (her) loveliness must surely mean that she
> excelled in gentle courtesy.

Canidia and Erichthoë were both famous Witches yet beautiful women. The great Hecate herself, though frequently described as of "terrible" appearance, is depicted as a beautiful woman on a stone carving in the British Museum, where she is to be seen with her sacred horse and dog.

Probably the most frequently referred to "wicked Witch" is the Bible's so-called "Witch of Endor." She is spoken of variously as an old hag, a crone, a diabolical woman of dark power…yet in actual fact there is nothing in the Bible to support these descriptions! She could have been young or old, beautiful or ugly. Nor is she even described there as a Witch! The Bible simply says that she is "a woman that hath a familiar spirit" (I Samuel XXVIII). It was King James's translators who, in 1611, added the heading "Saul Seeketh to a Witch," on the command of the king. We'll see how and why this happened later.

Where then, and why, did all this defamation come about? Why has the inverted, distorted image of the Witch been held for the past several hundred years? To find out we must return to the original question—what is Witchcraft?

The short answer is that Witchcraft is a religion. The longer, and more satisfactory, answer is to show the beginnings and the development of that religion. To do so we must go back twenty or thirty thousand years to the Paleolithic Age, where the God of Hunting first appeared.

In those times Nature was awesome, almost overwhelming to humankind. It was wonderful yet frightening. The rush and the roar of a waterfall, the twinkling stars, the powerful sun and bright moon, the sudden stab of lightning from an oppressive sky...it must almost have seemed that these things had minds of their own. They certainly had power. Out of awe, and respect, grew a belief in—for want of a better word—gods. A god controlled the gusting wind; a god was in the rushing, swirling river; a god swayed the mighty trees. This was *animism*—the most potent factor in the evolution of religion. Even today in some of the islands of the South Pacific, and elsewhere, a lingering of these beliefs can be found. For example, when about to chop down a tree a native will first tap three times on its trunk, to give the residing spirit time to get out.

Hunting, and success in the hunt, was of prime importance to the early people. Meat was needed for food, skins for warmth, bones to fashion into tools and weapons. Without these things a tribe would perish. When hunting, omens were sought to show that the hunt would be successful. Omens can multiply rapidly and become very involved. It seemed to these early people that some power controlled them. A God of Hunting? In order to have success in the hunt, then, it would seem desirable to gain the favor of this god, to have him direct the hunt as the hunters would have it go. The fact that when it came to it the hunt did *not* always go exactly as hoped seemed to indicate that this Hunting God was not always in an agreeable mood. Supplication might well be needed, it was felt.

Along with these first faltering steps of religion came *magick**. The earliest form of magick was almost certainly of the "sympathetic" variety—similar things, it was held, have similar effects; like influences like. Magick was used to direct the hunt. One man would play the part of the Hunting God, directing the others and thus supervising the magick. As the God of Hunting he would present himself much like the animal to be hunted, with the skin and antlers, or horns, of that creature. (Most of the animals hunted at that time were antlered, as we can see from contemporary cave paintings. It is here interesting to note that the majority of animals depicted in cave paintings were the food of humankind.) A model of the animal was fashioned from clay, or similar material, and set on the floor of the residential cave or in an open clearing. Under the priest's direction (for "priest" is what the god-player was, in effect) the simulated animal was attacked and "killed" by the hunters. Successful in this killing, it was then felt that they could go out and hunt the real animal and the hunt would be equally successful, going exactly as they had acted it before the god.

Evidence of this early religio-magick has been found in such places as the Caverne des Trois Frères at Ariége, France. Here

---

*The early spelling of the word is preferred to differentiate between it and stage conjuring, or illusion.

"The Sorcerer"

Caverne des Trois Frère, Ariége, France

can be seen the cave painting which has become known as "the Sorcerer." This shows the figure of a man dressed in the skin of a stag and wearing a mask and antlers. At Fourneau du Diable, Dordogne, is found another such figure, this time wearing the horns of a bull and playing some sort of musical instrument. At Le Tuc d'Audoubert, Ariége, is a very realistic clay model of a bison, pock-marked with holes where it was literally attacked with spears and javelins. There is also the similarly holed model of a bear. The bear, however, was modeled without a head. There is a hole in the neck where, presumably, a stake was placed from which hung a real bear's head. On a reindeer horn, discovered at Laugerie Basse, there is carved the prostrate figure of a man creeping on all fours toward a grazing bison.

Relatively recent illustrations of these rituals can be found in such examples as the Buffalo Dance of the Mandan Indians, in the Great Plains region of North America, where tribesmen were expected to keep a buffalo head in their tents to wear when the dance was performed. Deer masks were worn by the Penobscot Indians, and there were similar masks of the Eastern Woodlands tribes. A fine wood carving of a human head wearing antlers, worn at the Deer Ceremony, was found at the Spiro Mound, Oklahoma (1200–1600 CE).

By the Bronze Age horns had become a sign of divinity and horned gods were fairly common in areas such as Mesopotamia. The number of horns came to indicate the importance of the god, seven horns being the acme of divinity—hence the seven horns of the Divine Lamb of the Book of Revelations.

Alongside the Hunting God there was a Goddess—the Great Mother, Goddess of Fertility. For along with success in the hunt, fertility was of prime importance to early humankind.

Masked Dancer

Cave painting, Dordogne, France

Without plentiful game, there would be starvation. Without children to the tribe, the rigors of the time would efface it. Fertility was therefore necessary in both animals and humans, and again magick played a part. At Le Tuc d'Audoubert is also to be found a clay model of a male and a female bison mating. Sympathetic magick again, this time presided over by the Goddess. The power manifest in all forms of fertility was personified in her. Many figures, generally referred to as "Venus figurines," have been found depicting this Mother Goddess. One of the best known is the Gravettian figure of 20,000 years ago found at Willendorf, in Austria. With its bounteous breasts, belly, buttocks, and open vulva, it is the undoubted personification of fertility. The Venus of Laussel is another fine example, as is the Venus of Sireuil. Many others might be mentioned but all bear these same characteristics: the emphasis on the feminine attributes and the complete lack of identity in the face. There is ofttimes a shapeless lump for a head, or no head at all. The arms and legs may be well-formed, as on the Venus of Laussel, or they may be just barely suggested. At a later stage in humankind's development, with the coming of agriculture, the Goddess was to become the more important of the two principle deities, but for many years she was to reign beside the Horned God.

From studying the habits of present-day primitive peoples, such as the Australian aboriginals, the probable actions of early humans may be seen. In their painting of caves, for example, it was found—from actually filming them at work—that the painting was done as a ceremony in itself. The Headman, or priest, would officiate and there would be an audience, or congregation, who would join in ritual songs and dances at certain points in the work.

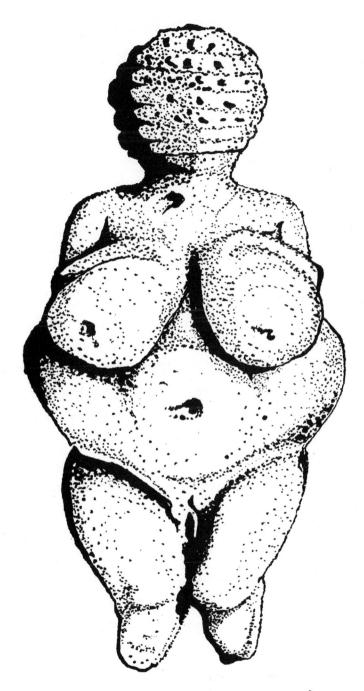

Gravettian "Venus" figurine (circa 18,000 BCE)
found at Willendorf, Austria

Drawing by Gerald Luxton, after B. Branston

In the Lascaux cave, among others, it is noticeable that a number of the paintings have been done in the most inaccessible places. The Sorcerer itself, as Murray points out (*God of the Witches*, Sampson Low Marston, London, 1931), can only be seen from that part of the cavern most difficult to get into. Was this the spot where the priest stood, as representative of the Hunting God, drawing inspiration from the painting? The artist must have had some sort of assistance to paint in that particular spot, definite indication that the paintings were not done for mere decoration but to serve a specific, almost certainly religious, purpose.

Dance and song, as an essential part of the religious hunting ceremony, is almost universal even today. The Yakuts of Siberia, for instance, and many Amerindian and Eskimo peoples, always dance before hunting. Dance/rhythm is the first step to *ekstasis*—the "getting out of oneself." When the dance is for the increase of food, the dancers frequently imitate the movements of the animals, or the growing of the plants, which they are trying to influence. As previously mentioned, the Masked Dancer at Dordogne is depicted playing some form of musical instrument. This might indicate a ritual similar to that of the primitive Semang, of the Malayan jungle, who today enact the hunting of the coconut ape through an action song. It is performed partly for entertainment but mainly for a magickal influence over the ape in a future hunt. The performance goes through the stalking of the ape to the actual killing, by blowpipe. An interesting point, however, is the inclusion in the song of the ape's feelings and the reactions of its family to its death.

The early cave rituals must have been tremendously impressive for, with the flickering of the firelight, it must almost have seemed to the participants that the animals painted on the walls were moving. This would lend credence to the idea of attacking and "killing" the clay figures on the cave floor.

So a crude form of religion came into being made up, as has been shown, of a combination of animism and magick. An essential part of magick is a belief in a supernatural force or power. The name usually given to this power is *mana*, a Melanesian word meaning "what inspires awe." The Australian *kutchi* could as well be used, as could *orenda* (Huron), *wakan* (Dakotah), or even the Hebrew term *Elohim*, which Huxley states "expresses something divine—that is to say, superhuman, commanding respect and terror" (*The Evolution of Theology—Science and Hebrew Tradition*). However, *mana* is the term generally favored. Extraordinary aptitudes of people are explained in terms of *mana*. The outstanding hunter, the great healer, the expert archer is better than the others because of possession of *mana*. Objects, too, can possess *mana*, as will be found particularly important in a much later development of humankind and magick. An unusually shaped stone will be treated as though possessing great magickal properties. A war club or a sword that renders its owner invincible holds great *mana*. But this *mana* can be controlled if one has the knowledge and the power. The one who has this knowledge and power is the magician or priest. He or she is the plenipotentiary between the ordinary people and the gods.

2: TO THE FOUR CORNERS

The early religion was, as has been shown, a polytheistic one with two major deities—the Horned God of Hunting and the Goddess of Fertility. That this Goddess was one of rebirth as much as birth is evidenced from the burial customs of the time, showing the belief in a life after death.

The practice of burial of the dead was an innovation of the Gravettians (22,000–18,000 BCE) who buried their deceased with their personal ornaments and in full clothing, sprinkling them with red ochre. Red ochre is a clay colored with hematite or iron peroxide, and because of its color it was (and still is among primitive peoples today) likened to blood. As the *Larousse Encyclopedia of Mythology* (Hamlyn, London, 1959) states:

> It is reasonable to suppose that the ochre spread over the tombs and bodies of Paleolithic man was

intended, like the deposits of food, to strengthen the dead one during his journey to the afterworld and his sojourn in his new abode.

How this belief in a life after death came about is not difficult to imagine. At the root of it are dreams. When a man slept he was, outwardly to his family and friends, like one of the dead. True, in sleep he occasionally moved and he breathed, but otherwise he appeared lifeless. Yet when he awoke he could tell of having been out hunting in the forest. He could tell of having met and talked with friends who really were dead. The others, to whom he spoke, could believe him, for they too had experienced such dreams. They knew he had not actually set foot outside the cave, but at the same time they knew he was not lying. It seemed that the world of sleep was as the material world. There were trees and mountains, animals and people. Even the dead were there, seemingly unchanged many years after death. In the other world, then, humans must need the same things they needed in this world. A man needed his spear, his axe, perhaps even his dog. These things, then, were buried with the body at death— all personal and treasured possessions. It would not do for a son to keep something which had belonged to his father, for it possessed the father's *mana;* it was essentially of the father.

A man-made trench, with a carpeting of red earth, houses three bodies at La Barma Grande. They are laid out side by side, heads resting on an ox-bone pillow, wearing their ornaments. These are of ivory and bone, shell, teeth, and fish vertebrae. There are also fine flint instruments beside and between them.

Initially graves were of two varieties: a plain earth grave or a stone, coffin-like structure surmounted by a heavy capstone.

Cromlech at Plas Newydd, Anglesey, Wales

The earth graves were frequently dug within the confines of the family cave. Under the hearth was a not an unusual place. There seemed to have been a feeling of wanting to keep the dead one still close to the family. Within these earth graves the body would frequently be lain in a fetal position, which would seem to be an indication of a belief in rebirth. It is also interesting to note that the majority of such graves were oriented east-west, with the head to the east. This is a point to bear in mind when considering the alignment of the modern Witches' altar (see Chapter 9). Later, in Neolithic times, large communal graves were used. Some of these cemeteries contained as many as two thousand bodies, each still accompanied by its personal possessions.

Towards the end of the Stone Age came the megalith builders, the builders of cromlechs, dolmens, and menhirs. Dolmens—single, table-like slabs supported by upright stones—were particularly common in Scandinavia. In Denmark and the lost provinces of southern Sweden, down to modern times, there were over 5,000 of them and they still stand in their thousands. The dolmen housed a body, or bodies, and was usually covered over with earth or small stones. It was a type of miniature chambered barrow.

The barrow itself was a burial mound of frequently tremendous size. The Lindeskov long barrow at Nyborg, Funen, in Denmark, is 550 feet wide and 1,150 feet in length. The barrow at New Grange, near Dublin, Ireland, is 45 feet high and over 200 feet long. As Jacquetta Hawkes says (*History in Earth and Stone*, Harvard UP, 1952):

> These tombs were far more than burial places… This becomes more acceptable when it is remembered that the cult associated with the tombs seems to have been no cult of the dead of a necrophilious kind but on the contrary one very much concerned with ideas of rebirth…The faith, for it is very truly a faith, which made the New Stone Age communities labor to drag, raise, pile thousands of tons of stone and earth, was in resurrection of their corn and beasts, of themselves. They laid their dead in the dark, earth-enclosed chamber with something of the same conviction with which they cast the seed corn into the soil.

This belief in a rebirth is given further emphasis when the form of these various barrows is considered. There is invariably a

Entrance to chamber at Uley, Gloucestershire, England

long, narrow passageway leading to a larger, rounded chamber which holds the body or bodies. This chamber is rarely located at the exact center of the mound but is usually some distance short of the center. It would seem probable that the chamber holding the dead actually represents the womb, with the passageway the symbolical vagina. This is further emphasized when studying the overall shape of some barrows, such as the one known as Belas Knapp in Winchcombe, Gloucestershire, England. The shape suggests a crude "gingerbread man" form, with the entrance to the barrow between the two stumpy legs. The fact that this is actually a "false entrance" does not detract from the general analogy; in fact, the "sealing-in" of the dead perhaps adds to it.

The most significant advance made during the evolution of culture was certainly the production of food based on the domestication of plants and animals. With the introduction of agriculture the Goddess came very much to the fore. Hunting was still necessary in the winter months, but for the greater part of the year the Horned God bowed to the Goddess, whose fertility had extended to crops as well as to man and beast.

Humankind soon spread from its origins, in the Fertile Crescent, across Europe and Asia. At the western extremity of the Fertile Crescent was the Valley of the Nile. Settlers were attracted to the banks of the Valley and developed agricultural settlements there. Although it had no great summer-winter change of season, the Valley did suffer from an inundation at regular intervals.

As humankind spread out, it took with it its gods, its budding religion, its beliefs and magick. The gods were to develop different names in different countries, but they were to remain the same basic deities. The religion was to take many different forms, and have different names in the various countries that developed. Yet it was always the same basic god and goddess, these deities of nature who had come into being and grown so naturally, as humankind had grown, who remained prominent everywhere.

The problem of names, when dealing with gods and goddesses, is a very real one. The deities of antiquity had an incredibly large number of names, many of them—the goddesses especially—having at least three different phases of themselves known by different names. For instance, the Great Mother might be worshiped in the likeness of a young woman, by a young man seeking success in love. She might be worshiped as a middle-aged woman, by a mother in pregnancy. She might also be worshiped as an old woman, by elders looking for knowledge and guidance. Each of these aspects of the Great Mother would have a different name, while she would have yet another secret name to her reg-

Roman altar stone of Cernunnos
Found beneath Notre Dame Cathedral

ular worshippers and a further most-secret name known only to her priests!

For all this the Great Mother always remains recognizable and, in the same way, the Horned God is recognized wherever he appears. There is an interesting dedication to be found carved into Hadrian's Wall, built 122–7 CE. It reads: "Aurelius Juvenalis (dedicates this) to the Mother-Goddesses of his own land over the sea."

The great nature god of the Kelts was *Cernunnos* (Latin: "the horned one"). He is found depicted on a stone altar discovered under the Cathedral of Notre Dame, in Paris. He is also on a beautiful silver cauldron, dating from the Iron Age, found at

Gundestrup, in Himmerland, Jutland. The imagery on this huge cauldron is Keltic: faces of the gods on the outside and animated scenes on the inside. Cernunnos is found in many parts of southern England, on a fourth century BCE rock-engraving in northern Italy, and on a Romano-Keltic sculpture now in the Cirencester Museum in England. In some parts of England he is Cernunnos, but in others his name has been shortened to *Cerne*. In yet other areas the name has become *Herne*. Indeed, "Herne the Hunter" is believed still to ride through Windsor Great Park, followed by his hounds, on nights of the full moon. Unfortunately few of the names of the indigenous deities of Britain have remained with us; the Romans Latinized the original names in their records.

Humankind was now living in organized communities. Thatched-roof houses of adobe, reeds, timber, or wattle-and-daub, were the more common types of dwelling. Larger and larger groups of people could be supported by a few acres of fields. When the community outgrew the land, another village was started elsewhere. Textiles were developed, as was pottery. With the development of agriculture there was a demand for grinding implements and provision for crop storage.

About 4,000 BCE objects made of copper began to appear in the Near East. At first all the objects were cold-hammered, but it was not long before smelting was discovered, followed by methods of casting. Then followed alloying—the fusion of two or more metals resulting in an alloy more malleable and stronger than any of its constituents. Alloying was first used to make bronze, which began to appear in quantity in Egypt and Mesopotamia about 3,000 BCE. This marked the start of what V.G. Childe termed the "Urban Revolution"—the invention of writing, money, the wheel, metallurgy, etc.

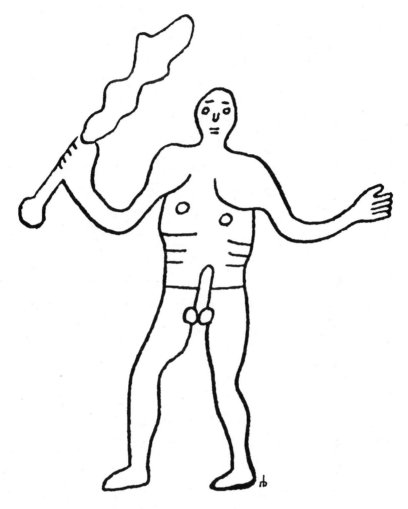

The Cerne Giant, Dorset, England

By the Bronze Age the Horned God was found across the whole of Europe, the Near and Middle East. Bull Dionysos and Pan (one of the many horned deities of the mainland of Greece) are two examples. The legend of Theseus and the Minotaur has been cited as another possible example involving the ritual sacrifice of a priest-king, representative of the Horned God. In the new cities temples were built to the gods, but in most places people got together to worship in the open.

At this point let us take a look at the Kelts and their priests, the Druids. The Kelts, or Celts, were a tall, fair people who occupied Central and Western Europe. They wore tunics dyed in many colors and the men carried shields as tall as themselves. Some wore breastplates into battle while others fought naked. Their helmets were usually of bronze and bore either horns or large figures of birds or beasts. Their swords were short and double-edged. They also used javelins and lances with iron tips. According to Poseidonius of Apamea, their appearance was awe-inspiring. They kept herds of sheep and a number of swine, from which they supplied pork and mutton to the Romans. They also traded in metals.

The Druids almost certainly arrived in Britain with the Kelts, about 500 BCE, though their origin is in some doubt. Lewis Spence (*An Encyclopedia of Occultism*, Routledge, London 1920) suggests a non-Keltic and even non-Aryan origin for them. He thinks it possible that the "so-called Iberian or Megalithic people of Britain introduced the immigrant Kelts to the Druidic religion." Certainly Britain became the center of the religion, the Isle of Anglesey being the chief seat.

The name "Druid" probably comes from the Gaelic word *Druidh*, meaning a "wise man" or "magician," though Lewis Spence (*The Magic Arts in Celtic Britain*, Rider, London) says: "...the name 'Druid' has been the subject of obstinate contention. Pliny the Elder interpreted it as referring to the Greek word *drus*, 'an oak'; Rhys finds the genesis in the ancient Gaulish Celtic name for that tree; George Henderson translates the word as *dru-vid* 'very wise,' Toland thought the word *drud*, in old

Foliate Mask

Representation of the old nature God, on a candelabra

British 'a discreet or learned person,'..." and so he goes on to mention a dozen other interpretations. Whatever the etymology, the Druids served as priests, doctors, judges, and teachers, their authority being, in most cases, supreme. According to Julius Caesar (*Gallic Wars*):

> The Druids...are concerned with divine worship, the due performance of sacrifice, public and private, and the interpretation of ritual questions... The cardinal doctrine which they seek to teach is that souls do not die, but after death pass one to another...beside this they have many discussions as touching the stars and their movements, the size of the universe and the earth.

Caesar tells how, in their schools, the Druids "learn by heart a great number of verses, and therefore some persons remain twenty years under training." In R.A.S. Macalister's *The Archaeology of Ireland* (Dublin, 1928) he suggests that the Irish Druids at least were learning sacred hymns dating from before the introduction of writing and, "like the Vedas in ancient India, preserved by oral tradition, because they would have been profaned were they to be committed to the custody of this novel art." At that time there was both Greek and the ancient Irish Ogham alphabet available and known by the Druids, so it was obviously from choice that the learnings were not written down.

The temples of the Druids were generally outdoors, situated in dense groves of oak trees. They were usually circular or oval in form. In the center was placed a large stone which represented the principle male deity. Polytheistic, the Druids had two main deities: one male and one female. This god and goddess probably bore the names Hu and Cerridwen, though this is by no means certain. Other possibilities are Lud and Deva. As is so often the case the most holy names of the gods were known only to the higher ranking Druids. According to Iolo Morganwg (*Barddas*, Llandovery, 1862), the word IAU is the "ineffable name of God," the most secret name that may be written but not spoken, since no man knows its sound. There is here a parallel with the Jewish belief that YHWH is the sacred Tetragrammaton, the unpronounceable and unknowable name of their god.

One of the main festivals of the Druids was May Eve, *Bealltainn*, or Beltane, as it is with Witches. On this date the Druids would light huge Beltane fires on the hilltops. Around the fires choral dances were performed in tribute to the sun. Other festivals were held at *Samhain* (November Eve) and at the Summer and Winter Solstices—again as will be seen with the Witches.

It is learned from Pliny that:

> The Druids esteem nothing more sacred in the world than mistletoe, and the tree whereon it breeds, so it be an oak...Mistletoe they gather very devoutly and with many ceremonies, because she is thought to be of great power and force sufficient...They call it in their language All-Heal (for they have an opinion of it, that it cures all maladies whatsoever), and when they are about to gather it, after they have well and duly prepared their sacrifices and festival cheer under the said tree, they bring there two young, milk-white bullocks...The priest, arrayed in a surplus or white vesture, climbs up into the tree and with a golden hook or bill cuts it off, and they beneath receive it ...then they kill the beasts, mumbling many

oraisons and praying devoutly...Now this persuasion they have of mistletoe thus gathered, that
whatever living creature (otherwise barren) does
drink of it, will presently become fruitful.

Tacitus, in his *Annals XIV*, describes the final collapse of
Druidic power, with Suetonius Paulinus leading the Roman
attack on the Druids at the island of Anglesey in 60 CE.

The early priesthood of Witchcraft was, in many ways,
similar to the Druids. The word "Witch" probably comes
from the Anglo-Saxon *wica*, or *wicca* (f. *wicce*), meaning
"wise one." The word "wit" comes from the same root. Wica
was the name originally given only to the priesthood of the
Old Religion, as it had developed in Western Europe and
elsewhere. At a later stage the name became used by all
adherents. Like the Druids, the Wica were truly the Wise
Ones. They had to be. As well as religious leaders they had to
be the community's doctors, lawyers, judges, farmers, and
hunters. They had to have knowledge in all things to advise
and lead their followers.

The religion whose early beginnings we saw in Chapter One
had developed to the point of having "form"—set rituals, festivals, a regular priesthood. But for all that it remained a *simple*
religion, a religion very much "of the people," as will be shown.
The two main festivals of the Wican year occurred at Samhain
(pronounced *Sow-'un*) and Beltane: November Eve and May Eve.
During the summer months, when food could be grown, the
Goddess was to the fore. But in the winter—the so-called "dark
half" of the year—the growing time was over and the Horned
God of hunting once more became prominent. The two festivals
occurred at, and signified, the changeover from one season to the

other. This, then—Nature and the turning of the wheel of the year—was the basis of the Old Religion…soon to come into sharp conflict with a new variety: Christianity.

3: THE RIVALS

There was not the immediate mass conversion to the New Religion that is so often suggested. Christianity was a religion which, in effect, started at the top; the rulers, townspeople, and upper classes were converted—though frequently only superficially—long before the working classes, villagers and country people. In fact as late as the eleventh century it was still very much in the balance as to which would finally triumph, the Old Religion or the New. An attempt at a mass conversion was made by Pope Gregory the Great. He thought that one way to get people to go to the Christian churches was by building them on the sites of the Old Religion's meeting places. Where there were already actual temples, these could be converted. In 601 ce, in a letter to Abbot Mellitus (Bede, *Ecclesiastical History of the English Nation*), who was about to journey to England, the Pope said:

When (by God's help) you come to our most reverend brother Bishop Augustine, I want you to
tell him how earnestly I have been pondering over
the affairs of the English: I have come to the conclusion that the temples of the idols in England
should not on any account be destroyed. Augustine must smash the idols, but the temples themselves should be sprinkled with holy water and
altars set up in them...For we ought to take
advantage of well-built temples by purifying them
and dedicating them...In this way, I hope the people (seeing their temples are not destroyed) will
leave their idolatry and yet continue to frequent
the places as formerly, so coming to know and
revere the true God. And since the sacrifice of
many oxen to devils is their custom, some other
rite ought to be solemnized in its place such as a
day of dedication or festivals for the holy martyrs
whose relics are there enshrined. On such high
days the people might well build themselves shelters of boughs round about the churches that
were once temples and celebrate the occasion with
pious feasting. There must be no more sacrifice of
animals to the Devil, but they may kill them for
food to the glory of God. (!)

It has frequently been said that the gods of an old religion
become the devils of the new. This was certainly the case so far
as Christianity was concerned. The Horned God of the Old Religion was immediately equated with the Christian Devil who, it
seemed, was also horned (cf. St. Augustine, *Enarratio in Psalmos*,
Psalm 96, v.5: *Omnes dii gentium daemonia*—"All the gods of the
heathens are demons").

The God of the Witches, from an Old Wood Carving
After C.G. Leland

It is interesting to note that the charge of "devil worship" lev-elled at the Witches is actually ridiculous. The Devil is a purely Christian invention, there being no mention of him before the New Testament. (The original Old Testament Hebrew *Ha-satan* and the New Testament Greek *diabolos* actually translate as "opponent" or "adversary" with no indication of an all-evil entity.) The Wica, therefore, by virtue of being a pre-Christian religion, do not even believe in the Devil, let alone worship him!

It transpired that the people were not quite as gullible as Pope Gregory thought them to be. When the first Christian churches were built the only workmen available to build them were still following the Old Religion. In building the churches these artisans incorporated carvings of their own gods into the decorations. On subsequently having to worship at these churches, they were then still able to worship their own much-loved deities rather than the new one forced upon them.

The figures of the gods, carved in wood and stone, were usually depicted as gods of nature, surrounded by leaves, fruit, nuts, etc. Ofttimes the head itself would be composed of foliage and for this reason most of these figures are referred to as "foliate masks," also "Jack o' the Green" and "Robin of the Woods." The Goddess was depicted as very much a fertility goddess, with greatly exaggerated breasts or with her legs spread wide displaying enlarged genitalia. Generally labeled "Sheila-na-gigs" a number of examples are still extant, most prominent being the one over the south door of Whittlesford's Church of St. Mary, in Cambridgeshire, and the one on the wall of the priory building at St. Ives, Huntingdonshire, England.

Even on the façade of the Colleoni Chapel in Bergamo, a work of the Renaissance, can be found alternating bas-reliefs depicting scenes from the Old Testament and from ancient mythology: the punishment of Adam and the Labors of Herakles. Of the same period is the base of the façade of the Certosa of Paria showing prophets, emperors, and ancient gods side by side. Here also Judas Maccabeus is depicted in a Mercury cap!

Goddess Figurine, Gloucester, England

By 250 CE the Christian religion in Rome itself numbered approximately 100,000 converts—including slaves—and in 313 CE was officially accepted by the Edict of Milan. In England Christianity ebbed and flowed. The concentration, as mentioned, was not on the general people but on the nobility. But in successive invasions of Danes, Norsemen, Angles, Jutes, and Saxons, the Old Religion received continual boosts. The records of the Christian ecclesiastics would show that Christianity was the only religion existing at the time, but it is illuminating to look at the short list of "conversions" that Margaret Murray gives (*The Witch-Cult In Western Europe*, London, 1921):

> 597–604: Augustine's mission. London still heathen. Conversion of Aethelbert, King of Kent. After Aethelbert's death Christianity suffered a reverse.
>
> 604: Conversion of the King of the East Saxons, whose successor lapsed.
>
> 627: Conversion of the King of Northumbria.
>
> 628: Conversion of the King of East Anglia.
>
> 631–651: Aidan's missions.
>
> 635: Conversion of the King of Wessex.
>
> 653: Conversion of the King of Mercia.
>
> 654: Re-conversion of the King of the East Saxons.
>
> 681: Conversion of the King of the South Saxons.

In the effort to establish the New Religion many old ideas were adapted. The Trinity, for instance, was a version of the old Egyptian Triad: Osiris-Isis-Horus becoming God-Mary-Jesus. The association of Mary with the Mother Goddess is obvious, but even the name of the Christian Saviour, Jesus, was not entirely new. A name frequently given to the old nature god of the Kelts was Esus, Consort of the Great Mother. As Pennethorne Hughes points out (*Witchcraft*, London, 1952):

> Many gods of the ancient world had been the offspring of Immaculate Conceptions, had had a childhood of danger, and had undertaken a mission which culminated in sacrifice for their people. They had died and risen again (in some cases as a

cultivation rite related to the rebirth of the year) and promised their followers salvation through their blood. The most obvious contemporary parallel was Mithras, from whose story most of the blood symbolism of early Christianity was derived.

In the middle of the fourth century the Church of Rome itself fixed the twenty-fifth of December (the birth date of Mithras) as the date of Jesus's nativity. Biblical evidence indicates quite plainly that Jesus was actually born during the late summer or fall, when Palestinian shepherds took their flocks to graze in the fields by night. To add to the confusion the Gospel of St. Matthew states that Jesus was born "in the days of Herod the king" and shows that at least two years later Herod was still alive. Yet it is well established in historical records that Herod died in 4 BCE. By this reckoning Jesus was born about 6 BCE!

However, Christianity stumbled on. In the seventh century the Archbishop of Canterbury prohibited sacrifices and eating and drinking in heathen temples. He gave penance to anyone who "at the Kalends of January goes about as a stag or a bull; that is, making himself into a wild animal, and putting on the heads of beasts." St. Caesarius of Arles, also in the seventh century, complained that:

> Some dress themselves in the skins of herd animals; others put on the heads of horned beasts; swelling and madly exulting if only they can so metamorphose themselves into the animal kind that they seem to have completely abandoned the human shape.

In 959 CE we see that the Old Religion was still alive and well for the Ecclesiastical Canons of King Edgar enjoined that:

> ...every priest zealously promote Christianity, and totally extinguish every heathenism; and forbid well worshipings, and necromancies, and divinations, and enchantments, and man worshipings, and the vain practices which are carried on with various spells, and with frithsplots, and with elders, and also with various other trees, and with stones, and with many various delusions, with which men do much of what they should not. And we enjoin, that every Christian man zealously accustom his children to Christianity, and teach them the Paternoster and the Creed. And we enjoin, that on feast days heathen songs and devils' games be abstained from.

The Christian William the Conqueror (1066 CE) did no great good for the New Religion by rendering waste nearly half of his new kingdom. His son and successor, William Rufus, an obvious follower of the Old Religion, was a "brutal tyrant without respect for Christianity," according to Archbishop Anselm. Yet according to Ordericus Vitalis (*Ecclesiastical History*, Bohn, London, 1847), "Rufus was imperious, daring and warlike, and gloried in the pomp of his numerous troops. The king's memory was very tenacious, and his zeal for good and evil was ardent. Robbers and thieves felt the terrible weight of his power, and his efforts to keep the peace throughout his dominion were unceasing." It seems the archbishop only considered him a "brutal tyrant" because he was against Christianity!

Dr. Fian, a Scottish witch, and his coven dance widdershins in the moonlight round as isolated country church.

The Old Religion, after so many thousands of years, so many generations of worshippers of the old gods, could not be stamped out. Many found themselves caught between the two religions. In 1280 the Abbot of Whalley was excommunicated for employing a "wise man" to "discover the body of his brother, drowned in the (River) Ouse." In 1282 a village priest, at Inverkeithing, in Scotland, was severely reprimanded for leading his parishioners in a fertility dance about a phallic symbol. The Bishop of Coventry, Walter de Langton, was himself accused, in 1303, of doing homage to a deity in the form of a goat. Pope Sylvester II, Pope Benedict IX, and Pope Gregory VII were all said to have "meddled in Witchcraft."

Slowly the *constructive* doctrines of the Old Religion were presented, by the Christians as *destructive*. Where the Old Religion's principle interest had been in the fertility of beast and crop, it now became blamed for famine and sterility, blight of beast and field. The old fertility custom of dancing around the fields astride poles at planting time (see Chapter 13) was presented, by the adherents of the New Religion, as a ritual to blight the crops. This was a singularly ridiculous charge, when studied, since the people so charged were the ones who had to live off those crops!

Yet many of the old rites did continue and quite a few have even survived through to the present. The Maypole dances, Morris dances, and other such festivities still practiced today are survivals of old Pagan rites.

In 1133 the monk Rudolf of St. Trond related how a countryman in the Rhineland built a huge wooden ship on wheels, representing the ship of the Earth Goddess Nerthus. With other men he hauled it to Tongres, Loos, Maestricht, and Aix-la-Chapelle where…

> …under the twilight of dawn crowds of matrons having cast away all feminine shame, loosened their hair, leapt about clad in their shifts, two hundred dancing round the ship shamelessly. You might see one hundred thousand people of both sexes celebrating into the middle of the night. When that execrable dance was broken off the people ran hither and thither making a noise as though they were drunk.

On May Eve the people would go out to search for flowers and green boughs, often staying out overnight. William Stubbs, the Puritan, commented (*Anatomy of Abuses*):

The huge Maypole set up in London. It stood for generations until,
in 1517, it was taken down and stored in a row of cottages until,
thirty-two years later, it was preached against and destroyed.

I have heard it credibly reported by men of great
gravitie, credite and reputation that of fourtie, thre
score or a hundred maides goying to the woode
ouer night, there have scarcely the thirde part of
them returned home againe undefiled.

The people's view is aptly summed up in Rudyard Kipling's words (adopted by modern Wicans as their *May Eve Chant*, and sometimes sung whilst dancing around the Maypole):

> *Oh, do not tell the priests of our rites*
> *For they would call it sin;*
> *But we will be in the woods all night*
> *A-conjurin' Summer in!*

The words *heathen* and *pagan* are frequently used to describe followers of the Old Religion. These names are by no means derogatory, as is so often implied. *Heathen* simply means "a dweller on the heath." Similarly, *pagan* (from the Latin *paganus*) means "one who dwells in the country." Since the town-dwellers were converted to Christianity before the country folk (who still live so much closer to the land, to Mother Earth), to call a person a pagan or heathen was simply to say that they lived "out of town," and therefore to infer that they still followed the Old Religion.

So for the first thousand years or more of Christianity the New Religion seemed content just to try to convert others to it. When, however, it became apparent that not all had been converted and not only that but that there were no longer any willing to *consider* conversion, then it was felt that firmer measures should be taken. Anything that was non-Christian was automatically labeled *anti*-Christian. And everything that was non-Christian was lumped together as the Devil's work: Satanism!

First one side would seem to be ahead, then the other. Finally Christianity grew impatient. It *must* win! If it could no longer convert—it would destroy! Full scale war was to be waged.

4: CRY HAVOC

"We, the Bishop of Sitie, Vicar-General of Monsignor the Cardinal of Lorraine at his bishopric in Toul, assign to you, Master Dominic Gordel, the afternoon of Friday April 26th for the continuation of the torture, that the truth may be known from your own mouth."

So was sentence pronounced "on one who is Defamed, and who is put to the Question" according to the *Malleus Maleficarum*.

> Some are so soft-hearted and feeble-minded [warns the *Malleus*], that at the least torture they will confess anything, *whether it be true or not.** Others are so stubborn that, however much they are tortured, the truth is not to be had from them. There are others who, having been tortured before, are the

---

*Author's italics.

better able to endure it a second time, since their arms have become accommodated to the stretchings and twistings involved; whereas the effect on others is to make them weaker, so that they can the less easily endure torture.

So the New Religion, Christianity, fought its battle, the battle that was really launched in earnest in December 1484 with the Bull of Pope Innocent VIII, two years before the publication of the *Malleus Maleficarum*. The Bull was a typical pronouncement from a Christian against a non-Christian form of worship having fertility as the central theme. It laid great stress on power over fertility, citing intercourse "that members of both sexes do not avoid to have…with demons, Incubi and Succubi." By this intercourse and sorcery general sterility of women, animals, corn, vines, trees, etc., was supposedly caused. Humans and beasts were tormented with pain and disease. "They hinder men from generating and women from conceiving; whence neither husbands with their wives nor wives with their husbands can perform the sexual act." The Bull continues, naming "our beloved sons Heinrich Kramer (Institor) and Jakob Sprenger, Professors of Theology, of the Order of Friars Preachers…delegated as inquisitors of these heretical depravities." All obstacles to the work of these inquisitors were requested removed. They were not to be molested or hindered by any authority whatsoever and "if any man dare do so, let him know that on him will fall the wrath of God Almighty and the blessed Apostles Peter and Paul."

Practically every pope during the fifteenth and sixteenth centuries had issued a Bull against sorcery. As early as 1235 Gregory IX, writing to the Archbishop of Sens, had said, "Thou shouldst be instant and zealous in this matter of establishing an

Inquisition by the appointment of those who seem best fitted for such a work, and let thy loins be girded, Brother, to fight boldly the battles of the Lord." Pope Alexander IV launched a Bull against Witchcraft in 1258. He followed this with a second in 1260. That the Bull of Innocent VIII assumed especial importance, however, was due to the rapid spread of printing at that time, and the resulting widespread distribution the Bull received.

It is interesting that the Church seemed so concerned about hindering "men from generating with women." It so happened that the Church itself had very strict rules governing such intercourse. There should be no joy in the act, it was declared, and it was only permitted for procreation. Celibacy was all but forced on the populous. As Brad Steiger points out (*Sex and Satanism*, Ace, New York, 1969):

> When the church proclaimed coitus illegal on Sundays, Wednesdays and Fridays it effectively removed the equivalent of five months of the year from the possible taint of sexual pleasure. Mother Church's next move was to enforce sexual abstinence for forty days before Easter and forty days before Christmas. Clerical decree had now removed the equivalent of nearly eight months from medieval man's coital calender. It furthermore seemed advisable to the clergy that sexual intercourse be prohibited for three days prior to receiving communion—and regular communion attendance was required. From the remaining four months available for permissible sexual intercourse, the new edict could remove the equivalent of at least one other month. Then, of course, coitus was forbidden from the time of conception

to forty days after parturition and any time during
any clerically levied penance.

This left a total of approximately two months in the year when
it was permissible to have relations with your spouse—though
only, of course, for the purpose of procreation and definitely without any feelings, or thoughts, of pleasure on the part of either!

What sort of person was Innocent VIII, that he gave the two
German monks *carte blanche* in their persecution of Witches?
Contemporary Catholic chroniclers recorded that the pope kept
a mistress, by whom he had two children: a son and a daughter.
He died at the age of sixty but, according to the records, he was
kept alive during his last months by sucking milk from a
woman's breasts. Russell Robbins, author of the heavily editori-
alized *Encyclopedia of Witchcraft and Demonology* (Crown, New
York, 1965), states that three young boys died as the result of
blood transfusions attempted to rejuvenate the pope. (It is interesting here to note that during the earlier part of the Middle
Ages there were no trained surgeons in Europe. The only men
with medical education were Jews who studied in Arabia.
Employment of these men was forbidden by the Church,
although its officials did not hesitate to consult them in cases of
their own serious illness.)

What sort of men were these who were made authors of this
infamous work? Heinrich Kramer was once a Witch-hunter in
the Tyrol. To achieve his ends it is said that he once bribed an old
woman to climb into a baker's oven and scream that the Devil
had put her there. She was then, from the oven, to name some of
the Devil's followers in the area. This the woman did and Kramer
played his game through to the bitter end. Seizing the women and

Some of the instruments of torture used in the Bamberg Witch trials

men named by his confederate, he put them to the most cruel of tortures in order to extract a "confession" from them. He would go to any lengths to see people burned as Witches.

The Bull of Innocent VIII was reprinted as a preface to the *Malleus Maleficarum* on its appearance in 1486. This gave great prestige to the book's two authors. The book was, however, the most sinister work ever published. It was to be used as the handbook for Witch-hunters and Judges for the next two hundred years. Divided into three parts, it dealt with (a) the need to thoroughly understand Witchcraft and to accept all evidence against it, whether or not normally acceptable; (b) the types of Witchcraft encountered and countermeasures that might be taken; and (c) the very precise rules governing the trials of Witches. The complete work is so illogical in its thinking and arguments, even for the time it was written, that it is amazing that it ever became the power that it did. One reason, perhaps, is that Kramer and Sprenger, for further prestige, forged the official letter of approbation from the Theological Faculty of the University of Cologne (the Official Censor of Books at that time). Joseph Hansen, the learned archivist of Cologne, actually exposed the forgery—which had long been suspected—in 1898. Apparently copies of the book actually sold in Cologne did not carry the Approbation, but it was in those circulated elsewhere. At Sprenger's death, in 1495, although he was a member of the Theological Faculty, he was not given the traditional Requiem Mass by the University.

Robbins describes the *Malleus* as "without question the most important and sinister work on demonology ever written." Pennethorne Hughes speaks of it as "a most hideous document. It defied all that we mean by the laws of evidence. It presumed guilt and it advocated torture."

It is certainly a terrifying testimony to the ways of the Church at that time. It details all the many tricks and tortures that were felt justified to obtain a confession, presuming that all charged with Witchcraft were necessarily guilty. The first part treats:

...the three necessary concomitants of Witchcraft which are the Devil, a Witch, and the permission of Almighty God.

Here the reader is first admonished that to *not* believe in Witchcraft is heresy. Points are then covered on:

...whether children can be generated by Incubi and Succubi; Witches' copulation with the Devil; whether Witches can sway the minds of men to love or hatred; whether Witches can hebetate the powers of generation or obstruct the venereal act; whether Witches may work some prestidigitatory illusion so that the male organ appears to be entirely removed and separate from the body; various ways [that Witches may] kill the child conceived in the womb, [etc., etc.].

The second part:

Treating of the methods by which the works of Witchcraft are wrought and directed, and how they may be successfully annulled and dissolved...The several methods by which Devils through Witches entice and allure the innocent to the increase of that horrid craft and company; the way whereby a formal pact with evil is made; how they transport from place to place; how Witches impede and prevent the power of procreation; how as it were they deprive man of his virile member; how Witch midwives commit most horrid crimes when they either kill children or offer them to devils in most accursed wise; how Witches—injure cattle, raise and stir up hailstorms and tempests and cause lightning to blast both men and beasts.

Then follow remedies for all of the above. The third part of the book is perhaps the most important, for it is here that the order of the trial is dealt with:

> Relating to the judicial proceedings in both the ecclesiastical and civil courts against Witches and indeed all heretics…Who are the fit and proper judges for the trial of the Witches?…The method of initiating a process; the solemn adjuration and re-examination of witnesses; the quality and condition of witnesses; whether mortal enemies may be admitted as witnesses.

Here we are told that:

> …the testimony of men of low repute and criminals, and of servants against their masters, is admitted…it is to be noted that a witness is not necessarily to be disqualified because of every sort of enmity.

We learn that, in the case of Witchcraft, virtually anybody may give evidence, though in any other case they would not be admitted. Even the evidence of young children was admissible. This third part goes on with:

> How the trial is to be proceeded with and continued, whether the Witch is to be imprisoned; what is to be done after the arrest; points to be observed by the judge before the formal examination in the place

of detention and torture; how she must be questioned; the continuing of the torture; how they are
to be shaved in those parts where they use to con-
ceal the Devil's marks and tokens; various means of
overcoming their obstinacy in keeping silence and
refusal to confess; the trial by red-hot iron; the manner of pronouncing sentence, [etc., etc.].

It is obvious from the above that the authors of the *Malleus
Maleficarum* had certain obsessions. A large number of the chapters are, for example, concerned with sexual aspects of Witchcraft. But, as Julio Baroja points out (*The World of Witches*,
London, 1964), it was not the theologians and scholastic
philosophers who were responsible for putting these obsessions
into practice. It was the law and lawyers, Catholic *and* Protestant, who made the greatest use of it from its first appearance
right through to the early eighteenth century. Indeed—frightening as it may be—many present-day evangelists and "born-
again" Christians loudly make many of these same charges
against Witches and anyone else they do not care for!

A fire, then, was kindled by Kramer and Sprenger. It blazed
up, got out of hand, and spread rapidly across Europe. And,
indeed, the kindest interpretation that may be put on many of the
acts that were to take place before that fire died out is that there
was some form of insanity—a hysteria—that gripped people with
supernatural force. As Robbins says, it "opened the floodgates of
the inquisitional hysteria." The word "Witch!" became a war-cry
for rich and poor alike. If one had a neighbor with whom one dis-
agreed, to murmur "Witch" in the right place would ensure
removal of that neighbor. A landowner with his eyes on another's
property could murmur "Witch" and end up owning all.

A number of unscrupulous people made a very comfortable living out of "Witch Hunting." Perhaps the best known was Matthew Hopkins, who travelled the southeast of England in the mid-seventeenth century. His father had been a Puritan minister, he himself an unsuccessful lawyer. After accusing Elisabeth Clarke, an old woman with one leg, of bewitching a tailor's wife, Hopkins was joined by John Stearne and Goodwife Mary Phillips, who served as assistants and searchers. Claiming to have a list of all the Witches in England, the trio charged high prices to "search them out" for the various village and town authorities. The average wage in those days was sixpence (about a nickel) a day. Hopkins charged twenty shillings (forty six-pences) for each Witch unmasked, and proceeded to unmask them by the dozen. After only a few months of this new-found, lucrative business, Hopkins proclaimed himself the "Witch-Finder General." Carried away with his success, Hopkins began thinking of himself as a benefactor to Christianity and, conse-quently, did not hesitate to accuse John Lowes, pastor of Bran-deston, of Witchcraft. Lowes had been pastor for over fifty years. He had, at age eighty, grown into a crotchety old man and did not get on well with his parishioners. They, for their part, seized the opportunity to destroy him. Hopkins and his assistants kept the parson awake for several days and nights, walking him up and down, until he was utterly exhausted and did not know what he was saying or doing. In this way did Hopkins secure from him a detailed confession to having sunk a boat full of sailors at Ipswich! By 1646 Hopkins' influence was on the decline and he retired from "the business." According to James Howell (*Famil-iar Letters*, 1648), in the two counties of Essex and Sussex alone nearly three hundred supposed Witches had been arraigned through Hopkins, and almost all of these had been executed. According to his assistant Stearne (*A Confirmation and Discovery of Witchcraft*, London, 1648), "the women (executed) farre exceeded the men in number."

There have been many estimates made of the total number of people who lost their lives during the persecutions. A generally accepted estimate is nine million. However, this is not nine million *Witches* who were executed. (And it certainly is not nine million *women* who were executed, though some writers incorrectly state it as so. The majority were women, yes, but there were also many men and children.) Of the nine million a very small proportion were actually followers of the Old Religion, but most were, in fact, devout Christians wrongly accused.

After a particularly severe winter, the Bishop of Treves decided that the severity had been caused by Witches. He didn't know who in the village was a Witch, so he ordered the whole village destroyed. His policy was: "Destroy them all!...The Lord will know his own!"

Of the many things done "in the name of the Lord" none seems more at variance with the teachings of a "Prince of Peace" than the torturings inflicted to obtain "confessions" from those accused. In England torture was supposedly forbidden by law. This did not mean, however, that no one was tortured. Keeping the accused from sleeping was a favorite of the English accusers, as was making them walk continuously, hour after hour. Another favorite was to tie the accused cross-legged to a stool and keep him there, without food, for several days and nights. As Theda Kenyon says, in *Witches Still Live* (1928): "The blackest chapter in the history of Witchcraft lies not in the malevolence of Witches but in the deliberate, gloating cruelty of their persecutors."

From the *Malleus Maleficarum* it was shown that the best way to prove Witchcraft, and especially the pact with the Devil, was through confession by the Witch herself. And to obtain that confession torture was necessary. This torture, incidentally, was not to obtain *a* confession, but to obtain *the* confession…the particular confession, specific answers to very specific questions.

Robbins points out that burning at the stake, as the ultimate punishment, was supported by the Italian Professor Bartolo, in 1350, when he applied to Witches the words of Jesus: "If a man abide not in me (i.e., the Catholic Church), he is cast forth as a branch…and men gather them and cast them into the fire and they are burned." One wonders what would be Jesus's reaction to this interpretation put on his words?

Many of the tortures employed are illustrated in engravings of the times. One such engraving shows thirty people imprisoned in a small room, chained together in pairs. Deprived of food, they eventually became delirious through hunger and began tearing each other to pieces. Other illustrations show people stripped naked and being dragged along a tightly-drawn rope which, acting like a saw, cut the body in two. Some were tied to stakes and had fires lit a short distance away so that they would burn very, very slowly. There was also disemboweling, eye-gouging, and flogging.

One common form of torture was the *stappado* (from the Latin *strappare*, to pull), a way of pulling the arms from their sockets. It was done by tying the victim's hands behind his back then passing the rope over a pulley in the ceiling. The torturers would haul on the rope, lifting the victim off the ground. They would then tie weights to the feet until the victim's arms came out of his sockets at the shoulders. Occasionally, to vary the pace, the victim would be hauled up into the air close to the ceil-

The rack

ing then allowed to drop, but stopping short of the ground. In the case of a woman who was pregnant it was considered great sport to actually drop her on her belly!

The thumbscrews were frequently employed, as were leg-vises (often called "Spanish Boots" because of their use in the Spanish Inquisition). The thumbscrews were, basically, small vises designed to crush not only the thumbs but also fingers and toes. The boots were of two types. One type was adjustable, again as a vise, so that they could be tightened on the legs until the bones were crushed. The other type were over-large metal boots. The feet would be placed in them and then boiling water or oil would be poured in.

Different areas had different ideas. Sometimes one area would change authorities and so different ideas would appear in the same area at different times. Robbins gives the example of Hagenan, in Alsace. Here a woman was accused firstly by Protestants, in 1573, and found not guilty. Four years later she was again accused but by then the judges were Catholic. This time she was tortured seven times until she "confessed," then she was burned at the stake.

In Hermann Loher's monumental (if only in title!) *Hochnotige unterhanige wemutige Klage der frommen Unschultigen* of 1676 there is depicted a priest blessing the instruments of torture before they were used on a prisoner. Methods of torture were numerous. Besides those mentioned above they included hanging, beheading, gouging of eyes, flogging, burning, disemboweling, stretching on the rack, pouring water into the stomach until it swelled and burst, ovens, squassation, red-hot pincers, and other more complicated tortures. These latter included trapping dormice under an upturned bowl on the prisoner's stomach, then lighting a fire on top of the bowl so that the dormice would try to escape the heat by burrowing. The list of tortures is almost endless and merely emphasizes the depths of depravity to which humans can sink.

Pope Alexander VI was perhaps the most infamous of popes and certainly would have done nothing to lessen the tortures generally used. He was only twenty-five years old when his uncle, Pope Calixtus III, made him a cardinal and shortly afterwards appointed him to the very lucrative office of vice-chancellor. After the death of Innocent VIII Alexander attained the papal throne in 1492—reportedly by bribery. At this time the revenue of the popes was much impaired, so he set himself to reduce the power of the Italian princes and, if possible, seize their possessions. To effect this end it is reported that he used the vilest means, including poison and assassination. He sold indulgences and set aside the wills of several cardinals in his own favor. Alexander's son and daughter were the infamous Cesare and Lucrezia Borgia, and he was the one who had the ceilings of the Vatican apartments decorated with frescoes depicting the story of Isis, Osiris, and Apis—unusual scenes for a pope's chambers.

Sir John Fortescue, writing in 1468 about the laws of France (*In Praise of the Laws of England*), says that:

> They choose rather to put the accused themselves to the rack till they confess their guilt...Some are extended on the rack till their very sinews crack, and the veins gush out in streams of blood: others have weights hung to their feet till their limbs are almost torn asunder and the whole body distorted: some have their mouths gagged to such a wideness for such a long time, whereat such quantities of water are poured in that their bellies swell to a prodigious degree, and then being pierced with a faucet, spigot, or other instrument for the purpose, the water spouts out in great abundance, like the whale...To describe the inhumanity of such exquisite tortures affects me with too real a concern, and the varieties of them are not to be recounted in a large volume.

Although both in Scotland and on the Continent the ultimate penalty was burning at the stake, in England—and also in America, in New England—the maximum penalty was hanging.

Politics, of course, could not be kept out of the accusing and counter-accusing that was so rife. The most famous example was the plot of Francis, Earl of Bothwell, together with the Witches of North Berwick, against King James VI of Scotland. Prior to discovery of the plot James had not thought that "Witch power" amounted to much. However he apparently changed his mind on learning the details of the plot, for he afterwards wrote his *Daemonologie*, which was to become the classic for British Witchhunters, Matthew Hopkins included. He also was heavily influenced by his brush with the powers of the Witches of Berwick to the point where he let it influence his translation of the Bible. In one place he labeled the "Woman of Endor" a Witch. In another place he translated *veneficor* ("poisoner") as though it were *maleficor* ("Witch"), giving the law "Thou shalt not suffer a *Witch* to live," rather than the correct "Thou shalt not suffer a *poisoner* to live."

Another victim of politics was Dr. Dietrich Flade, who for twenty years headed the secular courts, became Vice-Governor of Treves and later Rector of the University. He was burned as a Witch in 1589. Although according to his contemporaries Flade had won fame and favor among the princes of the empire, and had amassed a considerable fortune in the process, his superiors felt he hindered their influence. His superiors were the Jesuit-trained Suffragan Bishop Peter Binsfield and the Governor Johann Zandt. In spite of the reluctance of the theological faculty of Treves to advise the archbishop on how to proceed, and the unwillingness of the assessors and acting judge to try him, Flade's superiors forced the issue and the one-time sentencer of Witches became sentenced himself.

In England one of the favorite ways of testing a Witch was to "swim" her. This involved stripping the poor woman, tying the thumb of her right hand to the toe of her left foot and the thumb of her left hand to the toe of her right foot, then tossing her into

The swimming of a Witch—1612

a river or the village pond. The belief was that if she sank and was drowned then she must surely have been innocent. But if she floated then it was with the Devil's help, and she would be hauled out and taken to trial. Many times the woman would not be stripped and, consequently, the air in her clothing would keep her afloat, leading to belief that she must definitely be guilty! As a legal test, "swimming" was abolished as early as 1219, but being popular with the people it was still practiced unofficially as late as the eighteenth century.

Another test, though not used a great deal, was to weigh the Witch against the Bible of the parish church. These Bibles were of enormous size and weight. It was believed that true Witches would weigh less than the Bible. But large as the Bibles were, there were few suspected Witches who did not outweigh them, which is probably why this test fell out of favor.

As late as July 1737 two London magazines carried reports of a woman, suspected of being a Witch, who was swum three times, each time floating. She was then weighed against the Bible and the villagers were not a little relieved to find she did outweigh it, since they were beginning to think (at that late date) that they might have started something which they might not have been willing to follow through.

Typical of the hysteria that was happening all over Europe during the persecutions was the Salem, Massachusetts, "Witchcraft outbreak" of 1692. So typical is it of what was sweeping across Europe at that time that we will give it a chapter to itself.

5: NEW ENGLAND'S TRIALS AND TRIBULATIONS

Before the Salem case of 1692 there were a dozen or so other cases of Witchcraft, with half a dozen executions, in Massachusetts. When it is realized that the exodus of Puritans to New England occurred during the reign of Charles I, while the persecutions for Witchcraft were ever on the increase in Great Britain, it seems unusual that there should have been so few cases in the New World.

When the Independents came over to New England they thought of themselves as entering the very domain of the Devil. They believed that all Pagan countries were under the jurisdiction of Satan and there was the added evidence, in the case of New England, of the Native American. Obviously, to them, the "red Indian" was one of Satan's imps! With this in mind, then, it is strange that instances of Witchcraft were so rare in New England's history.

The first victim of whom there is record was a Margaret Jones of Charlestown. She was hanged in 1648, for dispensing herbal cures. Another early victim was Mistress Ann Hibbins, sister of the Deputy-Governor of Massachusetts. She had a very high social standing, which makes the case an unusual one. The Colonial records do not show exactly what she was charged with; they merely contain the verdict and death warrant. The Rev. John Norton, the persecutor of Quakers, is on record as having said that Ann Hibbins was hanged "only for having more wit than her neighbors." This wit took her to the gallows on Boston Common in 1656.

In 1688 came the case of the Goodwin children. It involved a Catholic Irishwoman named Glover, who was laundress to the Goodwin household; John Goodwin and his wife; 13-year-old Martha; and three other children aged eleven, seven, and five.

One day Martha accused Goody (Goodwife) Glover of stealing some linen. The woman broke out in a burst of profanity and curses at the child, who very soon fell down in a fit. The other children quickly followed her example. Then the children went through all sorts of pranks. They would pretend to be deaf and dumb, then they would suddenly start barking like dogs. They would try to levitate themselves, moving quickly over the ground on their tip-toes so that Cotton Mather later said they could "fly like geese." They would also complain of being pricked by pins.

After a week or two of this behavior it was decided by the ministers who examined them that the children had been bewitched by the Glover woman. The Rev. Joshua Moodey wrote from Boston to Increase Mather (father of Cotton), who was then in England. He said: "We have a very strange thing

Cotton Mather

among us, which we know not what to make of, except it be Witchcraft, as we think it must needs be."

In fact they felt so strongly that "it must needs be" Witchcraft that they hanged Goody Glover. Cotton Mather, who had come in contact with the case at quite a late stage, took young Martha Goodwin into his home and kept her there for several months, to study her and treat her both medically and by prayer (Cotton

Mather was also a medical doctor). He said, in *Magnalia* (1700), "I took her home to my own family, partly out of compassion to her parents but chiefly that I might be eye-witness of things that would enable me to confute the *Sadducism* of this debauch'd age." He published a full account of the case in his book *Memorable Providences Relating to Witchcrafts and Possessions* (Boston, 1689).

John Fiske describes what happened in the Mather home (*New France and New England*, 1902):

> The girl showed herself an actress of elf-like precocity and shrewdness. She wished to prove that she was bewitched, and she seems to have known Mather's prejudices against Quakers, Papists, and the Church of England, for she would read Quaker books and Catholic books fluently, and seemed quite in love with the Book of Common Prayer, but she could not read a word in the Bible or any book of Puritan theology, or even in her favorite prayer book. Whenever she came to the Lord's Prayer she faltered and failed. Gradually the young minister's firm good sense and kindness prevailed in calming her and making her discard such nonsense, but during the cure her symptoms showed the actress.

Mather wrote that: "She went on Fantastick Journeys to the Witches' Rendezvouse." Actually she sat astride a chair and rocked backwards and forwards as though riding a horse. In his later book, *Wonders of the Invisible World*, Mather wrote: "The Witches say that they form themselves much after the manner of Congregational Churches."

The Goodwin children, as later with the children of Salem, knew exactly how a Witch was supposed to behave. Tracts and chapbooks on the subject were plentiful. The latest trials in England would be published, in detail, and very soon found their way across to the New World. Fiske wrote:

> In 1692, quite apart from any personal influence, there were circumstances which favored the outbreak of an epidemic of Witchcraft. In this ancient domain of Satan there were indications that Satan was beginning again to claim his own. War had broken out with that Papist champion, Louis XIV, and it had so far been going badly for God's people in America. The shrieks of the victims at Schenectady and Salmon Falls and Fort Loyal still made men's blood run cold in their veins: and the great expedition against Quebec had come home crestfallen with defeat. Evidently the Devil was bestirring himself; it was a witching time; the fuel for an explosion was laid and it needed but a spark to fire it. That spark was provided by servants and children in the household of Samuel Parris, minister of the church of Salem.

The town of Salem itself was not the scene of the outbreak. It was the village of Salem (later known as Salem Farms and today called Danvers). The name "Salem," of course, came from "Jerusalem." It was here that, in late 1689, the Reverend Samuel Parris came with his wife, his seven-year-old daughter Betty, his nine-year-old niece Abigail Williams, and his two black servants, Tituba and her man John Indian.

Before turning his attention to theology, Parris had lived some years in Barbados, where he acquired his two servants. It was after some argument that he took the position of minister to the parish, for it had a reputation for miserliness when it came to supporting its pastor. An entry in the church records, dated June 18, 1689, states:

> It was agreed and voted by general concurrence, that for Mr. Parris his encouragement and settlement in the work of the ministry among us, we will give him sixty-six pounds for his yearly salary—one third paid in money, the other two third parts for provisions, etc., and Mr. Parris to find himself firewood, and Mr. Parris to keep the ministry-house in good repair; and that Mr. Parris shall also have the use of the ministry-pasture, and the inhabitants to keep the fence in repair; and that we will keep up our contributions...so long as Mr. Parris continues in the work of the ministry among us, and all productions to be good and merchantable. And if it please God to bless the inhabitants, we shall be willing to give more; and to expect that, if God shall diminish the estates of the people, that then Mr. Parris do abate of his salary according to proportion.

The agreement was far short of what Parris wanted but in the end he agreed to it. There was a later violent disagreement when an entry in the parish book, voting to make over the real estate to Parris, was found and thought to be fraudulent. It was not signed by the clerk and in the ensuing quarrel many people refused to pay their church-rates. It was not a happy community!

Tituba and John Indian did most of the work about the house, of course. At times Tituba, who was not overly energetic, would put young Betty and Abigail to work, for they were frequently left under her supervision. But the girls were smart; they knew how Tituba loved to talk about her life in the West Indies. They found it a simple matter to get her to sit at the kitchen table with them, perhaps with young Betty on her knee, and tell them fascinating tales of the islands. Frequently they were not alone, for they could not help boasting to their girlfriends of this prize possession of theirs. The parsonage kitchen very quickly became a regular meeting-place for the village girls. This was especially true during the winter months when there was so little to do, for even the festivities of Christmas were denied a Puritan community; it had no place on their calendar.

Exactly what sort of stories Tituba told the children is not known for certain, though it is highly probable that they were heavily flavored with tales of Voodoo and magick. It is not unlikely that the children would try to re-enact some of these stories, perhaps even to the extent of going into simulated trances and uttering mystic words.

Besides Betty and Abigail the group of children included Ann Putnam, aged twelve, and Mary Walcott and Elizabeth Hubbard, both aged seventeen. There was also Elizabeth Booth and Susannah Sheldon, eighteen, and Mary Warren and Sarah Churchill, twenty. Occasionally they were also joined by Mercy Lewis, seventeen, a servant in the Putnam household.

Young Ann Putnam rapidly became the leader of the group, despite her age. She had a mother, also named Ann, who was well-educated but very highly strung. This was mainly through losing a number of children at birth before finally bearing the younger Ann. Her sister also had suffered in this way, finally dying in childbirth, and thoughts of those lost were forever in the older Ann's mind. Her daughter she used as a go-between to try to contact the dead in some way through Tituba.

Early in January 1692 young Betty started to have what could only be described as mild fits. She would stare into space for long periods then, when reprimanded, would cough and splutter and make sounds almost, so Parris said, like the barkings of a dog. Soon Abigail started doing the same, occasionally going to the extent of getting down on all fours and crawling through the furniture. The Reverend Parris prayed over the two girls, but since it seemed to do no good he finally took them to the village doctor. Doctor Griggs examined them as well as he was able but could find no reasonable explanation for their behavior.

Voodoo, as practiced in the Caribbean, is a polytheistic religion. It has its priesthood; it has its set forms of worship. One of the tenets of the religion is that the gods, known as the *loa*, can manifest themselves by taking possession of the worshippers. The chief deity is Damballah-Wédo, who is a serpent god. If one of the worshippers is possessed, or "ridden" by Damballah, then he or she will crawl on the ground and hiss like a snake. It is more than likely that Tituba described such possessions to the girls of Salem Village. Thoughts of such possessions may well have played on the mind of young Betty, at that time just nine years old. Not being familiar with snakes, she might have imagined being possessed by something she knew well, such as a dog.

Dr. Griggs knew nothing of Tituba's tales, or of Voodoo. He shrugged his shoulders in despair and ascribed the whole thing to Witchcraft.

"Someone," he said, "has obviously bewitched these girls!"

The Reverend Parris called in the elders of the village that they might pray over the girls. No one seemed to notice that whenever the girls had their "fits" they would merely indulge in all the high-spirited things which were normally forbidden to young ladies of such a community. They would shout and scream; they would roll on the floor or jump on the furniture; they would throw things about the room, including the Bible. In short they would "have a ball"! It was not long before their friends—those others of the Tituba circle—decided to join in the fun. The village was aghast to suddenly find itself with half a dozen or so hysterical girls on its hands.

This was all very well for a while but if, as seemed likely, the girls were truly bewitched, the distressed elders wanted to know who was causing the outbreak. People recalled the case of the Goodwin children. Mather's book on this had received wide circulation and there was probably a copy of it in the Parris household.

Parris called in clergymen from the surrounding countryside. They flocked to see the girls, who became known as the "Afflicted Children." The girls, for their part, must have realized that they had gone too far. But how, now, to stop? To admit that they were shamming would be to lay themselves open to beatings, embarrassment to their elders, to the clergy…it did not bear thinking about. They continued the pretense. And still they were being urged to name who afflicted them.

The Reverend Nicholas Noyes arrived in the village from the First Church in Salem Town. John Hale came from nearby Beverly. Hale had previously dealt with one or two cases of Witchcraft in his own area, but had been loath to act against it each time. For the gatherings of ministers the girls would put on a tremendous show. Abigail Williams especially rose to the occasion. Obviously relishing the limelight, she would howl louder than all the rest as the clergy tried to pray for them. Since the girls had not, apparently, been able to name who afflicted them, the ministers resorted to naming those who had any sort of notoriety in the area, to watch the girls' reactions. It seemed to have no effect. The girls continued their fits, the clergy their prayers.

It could not continue indefinitely. The girls had to name someone. Finally it was young Betty Parris who mentioned the name of Tituba, though whether she intended it as a charge or not is not known. Parris and the others leapt at the name. Was it Tituba? Other girls agreed that it was and, now that names were to be given, added those of Goody Osburn and Goody Goode ("Goody" being short for "Goodwife").

Sarah Goode had a bad name in the village. She was virtually a beggarwoman, her husband hiring himself out as a casual laborer. Sarah smoked a pipe, had a quick, coarse tongue, and during a recent smallpox epidemic had been accused of spreading the disease through her general uncleanliness and negligence. She had a number of children and was in fact pregnant at the time of her arrest.

Sarah Osburn was recently bedridden but, again, had no good name in the village. As a widow she had lived with her second husband, William, a number of years before marrying him. With the arrest of these three, and their removal to Ipswich Prison, the village started to breathe again. But it was not to be for long.

The preliminary hearing, to determine whether or not the case was worthy of a trial, was to be held in the village at Deacon Ingersoll's Ordinary. As it turned out, the capacity of the crowd exceeded that of the Deacon's room, so the meeting had to be held in the church. The magistrates were Jonathan Corwin and John Hathorne (an ancestor of the novelist Nathaniel Hawthorne). Neither of these men had any legal training, for the professional practice of law was not permitted in the Puritan colony. Before embarking upon the hearing, therefore, both men perused Cotton Mather's recent work on the Goodwin case and one or two other books, such as Bernard's *Guide to Jurymen* and Glanvil's *Collection of Sundry Tryals in England*.

On searching through the Bible they were no doubt nonplussed to find that nowhere in it was there given a definition of Witchcraft. In fact the word "Witch" itself was hardly used, especially in editions predating the King James version.

The accused were not legally represented in any way and were presumed guilty before the start. The hearing commenced on Tuesday, March 1st, and the first to be interviewed was Sarah Goode. She was openly defiant, disclaiming any knowledge of the affair. Several people testified, however, that there had been times when Goody Goode had come begging and been turned away. On leaving she had been seen to mutter to herself. A day or so later a chicken would have died or a cow run dry of milk. This seemed proof conclusive.

Goody Osburn was obviously a sick woman. She had been taken from her bed to the prison and now required assistance to get her to court. She was able to give little in the way of testimony, though whenever she looked at the "Afflicted Children," who were present, they would start going into fits. Finally Goody Osburn was removed and Tituba brought in. This caused a tremendous outburst from the children. It may well have been that they were afraid she would give the full story of the clandestine meetings in the Parris kitchen, that people would put two and two together and decide the girls were pretending. The girls need not have worried.

Tituba rose to the occasion magnificently. Far from claiming innocence, she admitted all with which she had been charged... and more! For three days she held forth telling her audience everything she felt it wanted to know. Certainly she was a Witch! As was Goody Goode and Goody Osburn. She had been approached by a man—a "tall man from Boston"—who wanted her to sign her name in his book. Goode and Osburn already had their names in the book, she said. There were, she added, nine names there altogether. This caused quite a stir in the court. If there had been nine names in the book, then there were other Witches still on the loose, waiting to be caught!

The trio was removed to Boston where, a few weeks later, Sarah Osburn died. Goody Goode had the child she was carrying when she was arrested, but it too died in the cell. Parris's wife insisted on sending Betty to stay with friends in Salem Town, for the fits seemed to be making her weak. This separation of the girls had the ultimate effect of curing Betty of her "possession."

John Proctor managed, briefly, to cure his servant Mary Warren of her affliction. His method was to set her to her work and promise her a beating if she left it for one moment, fits or no fits! He was most perturbed when Mary was finally called back to court, over his protests, by the magistrates. The elders and ministers had returned to praying over the girls and questioning them regarding the identities of the rest of the Witches. It was not long before Ann Putnam provided the name of Martha Corey, an outspoken woman who had moved to the village from Salem Town only the year previously. The main reason for suspicion, in her case, seems to have been her outright—and outspoken—disbelief in Witchcraft. When brought before the magistrates Martha started out firmly denying all and saying that the girls should be ignored. But everything that Martha did, the girls copied. If she bit her lip they would bite theirs till the blood ran, and say that she caused them to do it. One of the girls

The Rebecca Nurse home, Salem Village (Danvers), Massachusetts

claimed to be able to see "the Black Man" standing beside the woman and whispering in her ear.

The next to be "cried out upon" by the girls—once again led by Ann Putnam—was the aged, extremely deaf, Rebecca Nurse. Rebecca was in her seventies and had for almost a year been ill and confined to her bed. Her whole life, however, she had been regarded as one of the most respected of women, a veritable pillar of the community, a staunch and ever-devout Christian. The main charge against her was that while she lay seemingly immobile in her bed, her "shape"—her etheric double—was dashing about the community wreaking havoc...or so claimed the "Afflicted Children"! At Rebecca's trial a paper was produced, signed by thirty-nine people, attesting to her good character. It was to have no effect on the final outcome.

The children had their usual fits while Rebecca was being questioned. At one point, when Magistrate Hathorne seemed affected by her straightforward answers, Ann Putnam Senior cried out: "Did you not bring the Black Man with you? Did you not bid me tempt God and die? How often have you eaten and drunk your own damnation?" Rebecca raised her hands to heaven in despair and the girls took this as a signal to have violent fits. Hathorne decided that it was Rebecca's raised hands that had caused the fits, and she was sent to jail to await trial.

Thereafter arrests went on with increasing rapidity until, by the end of spring, at least one hundred twenty-five people were in prison. Among these were John Proctor and George Jacobs, masters to two serving-girls who were among the "afflicted." John Willard was another in prison. He had said that it was the girls who were the real Witches and deserving of the gallows. He was instantly cried out upon.

Perhaps the most amazing arrest was that of the Reverend George Burroughs. He had been minister in Salem Village from 1680 to 1682 and had left there because of various feuds within his church. To his later sorrow he had been on the opposite side of the feud to the senior Ann Putnam. He had settled in Wells, Maine, and was arrested there at the beginning of May and taken to Salem to answer the charge of Witchcraft. In a prior consultation with other ministers it came out that he had only had his eldest son baptized and that he couldn't remember when he had last served the Lord's Supper. Damning evidence! He was stripped and searched for the Devil's Mark, but without success.

By the middle of May the first Royal Governor, Sir William Phips, had arrived with a new charter, replacing the provisional government of Massachusetts that had followed the overthrow of

Andros. On Sir William Phips's orders, after issuing which he departed again for a few months, a special court of Oyer and Terminer* was appointed to try the Witchcraft cases. This was presided over by William Stoughton who, with Samuel Sewall, joined Hathorne and Corwin.

The evidence brought against Burroughs came mainly from Ann Putnam. He was charged, among other things, with murder —but of a "spectral" nature. Apparently whenever a soldier from the village had died in the Indian fighting he, Burroughs, had actually been responsible! His first two wives appeared—in ghostly form, visible only to the children—to testify that he had murdered them. Burroughs had always been unusually strong for his size and this was now held against him. Whereas he used to take pride in such a feat as that he "held out a gun of seven feet barrel with one hand, and had carried a barrel full of cider from a canoe to the shore," all this was now brought as evidence of his dealing with the supernatural.

One of the tests given to the Witches was the test of touch. As the "afflicted" writhed and screamed, the accused would be made to touch them. If the screaming then ceased it was proof of guilt, for the evil had returned, if only momentarily, to the accused. The test was frequently carried out and unfailingly proved the guilt of the one involved.

On June 2nd Bridget Bishop became the first of the accused to actually go to trial. Since her original hearing she had been chained up in a prison cell, seeing more and more of the accused join her. One of these was little Dorcas Goode, the five-year-old daughter of Sarah Goode. She, too, had been cried out upon by the girls and she, too, was chained, as was the custom with Witches.

---

*Meaning "to hear and determine"

Although the original examinations had been, supposedly, mere preliminary hearings, the evidence from them was carefully reviewed and noted by the magistrates of the Court. The only new business was the hearing of anything fresh which had been uncovered since that time. Bridget Bishop had been a tavern-keeper, having two ordinaries, one at Salem Village and the other in Salem Town. The main charge against her seems to have been that she wore a "red paragon bodice" and had a great store of lace. The "new" evidence against her was that she seemed to keep her youth despite her years. Various supposedly decent, upright, married men of the community testified that she had sent her "shape" to plague their sleep at night!

The afflicted testified that Bridget had been at the Sabbat meetings of the Witches and had, in fact, given suck to a familiar in the form of a snake. She was taken out and searched for a supernumerary nipple, which they claimed to find between "ye pudendum and anus." The verdict was a foregone conclusion. On June 10th Bridget Bishop was hanged on Gallows Hill.

There was then a break of twenty-six days while the judges argued over the pros and cons of accepting spectral evidence—the evidence of the afflicted saying that they saw the shape of the accused in a certain place when physically they were elsewhere. The concensus was that the devil could assume the shape of innocent people (this had previously been doubted) as well as of the guilty.

Rebecca Nurse's case soon came up and the jury returned a verdict of not guilty. There was immediately a great uproar, and the judges expressed their dissatisfaction with the verdict. The foreman of the jury later wrote, on a certificate, "When the verdict not guilty was given, the honored court was pleased to

The Rebecca Nurse grave and monument,
Salem Village (Danvers), Massachusetts

object against it, saying to them, that they think they let slip the words which the prisoner at the bar spoke against herself, which were spoken in reply to Goodwife Hobbs and her daughter, who had been faulty in setting their hands to the devil's book, as they had confessed formerly. The words were, 'What do these persons give in evidence against me now? They used to come among us!' After the honored court had manifested their dissatisfaction of the verdict, several of the jury declared themselves desirous to go out again, and thereupon the honored court gave leave; but when we came to consider the case, I could not tell how to take her words as evidence against her, till she had a further opportunity to put her sense upon them, if she would take it…these words were to me a principle evidence against her."

So after having had their verdict of not guilty rejected, the jurors retired once more and came back with a verdict of guilty. Rebecca tried to explain that when she had referred to Deliverance Hobbs—who had previously confessed to being a Witch, though she later joined the ranks of the afflicted—as being "one of us" she did not mean "one of us Witches" but "one of us prisoners"! It was to no avail. Earlier she had damned herself due to her deafness. She had not answered one of the questions put to her. She had just not heard it. But her silence was taken as acknowledgement of guilt. The Reverend Noyes excommunicated her and Tuesday, July 19th, in company with Sarah Goode, Elizabeth How, Sarah Wild, and Susanna Martin, she was hanged on Gallows Hill.

On August 19th the cart driven out to Gallows Hill carried five more: John Procter, John Willard, Martha Carrier, George Jacobs Senior, and the Reverend George Burroughs. Burroughs had been identified by the "Afflicted Children" as the "Black Man" in charge of the coven. He was allowed to address the crowd from the scaffold. This he did in carefully chosen words which worked on the emotions of the crowd. So much so, in fact, that some started to call for his release. One of the tests of a Witch was that he or she could not say the Lord's Prayer without blundering. George Burroughs stood at the scaffold and, clearly and faultlessly, recited it to the crowd. Almost certainly they would have released him but, as some moved forward, a young man on a horse cried out to them to stop. It was Cotton Mather. With stern words he cautioned them against the workings of the Devil, intimating that it had been the Devil speaking to them through Burroughs. The hanging went on as planned.

On Monday, September 19th, an unusual execution was carried out. When a man is brought before the court for trial he is first required to plead whether he is guilty or not guilty. No trial can proceed until the accused has so pleaded. By refusing to plead, therefore, the accused can prevent the trial altogether. To circumvent such an occurrence the law provided a horrible punishment for anyone so obstinate. This was called *peine fort et dure*, which means, literally, "a penalty harsh and severe." It consisted of stretching out the culprit flat on his back, with his arms and legs extended to the utmost in four directions. Heavy weights of iron and stone were then piled on the body till he either pleaded or died. The common name for this process was "pressing to death."

Giles Cory was arrested for Witchcraft in April. His wife, who had been in jail since March, was sentenced to death on September 10th, and his own trial came two or three days later. In all his eighty years Giles had never known the meaning of fear, yet seeing what was done to his wife nearly broke his heart. He knew that if he did not plead not only would the trial be baulked but also the authorities would be unable to confiscate his goods and estate, as they would be able to do should he be proven guilty. Giles therefore refused to plead and was, subsequently, put to the *peine forte et dure*—the only time in American history that this punishment has been inflicted. Giles Cory was finally pressed to death, but he never did plead.

Eventually the accusers went too far. They started mentioning members of the Mather family; they tried to implicate Lady Phips, wife of the Governor; they named the most respected Reverend Samuel Willard and, finally, Mrs. Hale, wife of John Hale himself. This was too much. These accusations opened the eyes of John Hale to the point where he turned right about and began to oppose the whole prosecution. He confessed that he had been wrong all along. It seemed that a number of people had reached similar conclusions. More and more ministers came out with Hale against the prosecutions. The court recessed.

A fatal blow to the Witch-hunters came when a group of people in Andover, on being accused of Witchcraft, retorted by bringing an action of defamation of character with heavy damages. This marked the end of the panic.

Just at this time the court of Oyer and Terminer was abolished due to the assembly of the General Court of Massachusetts at Boston. It was the first court elected under the new charter. The jail at Salem was filled with prisoners and many had to be taken to other jails. When the court met for the first time in January 1693, it started by throwing out indictments. The grand jury found bills against about fifty for Witchcraft, but upon trial they were all acquitted. Some of the court were dissatisfied, but the juries changed sooner than the judges.

In May 1693, Governor Phips ordered the release from jail of all those awaiting trial, and the Salem Witchcraft hysteria was past. Excommunications were erased and claims from survivors and those who had been held from days to months, awaiting trial and almost certain death, were honored by the colony within a few years.

Five years afterwards Judge Samuel Sewell stood up in the Old South Church and publicly acknowledged his shame and repentance. For the rest of his life he kept a day of fasting and prayer, every year, in memory of his errors. Ann Putnam, the younger, fourteen years afterwards, stood before the congregation of Salem Village Church and confessed that she, and others, had been the cause of bringing upon the village the guilt of innocent blood, "though what was said and done by me against any person, I can truly and uprightly say before God and any man, I did not out of any anger, malice, or ill-will to any person, for I had no such thing against one of them, but what I did was ignorantly, being deluded of Satan. And particularly as I was a chief instrument of accusing Goodwife Nurse and her two sisters, I desire to lie in the dust and to be humbled for it, in that I was a cause, with others, of so sad a calamity to them and their families."

What happened in the little village of Salem, where nineteen people were hanged and one man was pressed to death, was as nothing to what happened in Europe throughout the persecutions as the New Religion, Christianity, tried to suppress and destroy any and all it thought to be non-Christian.

The last official trial for Witchcraft in England was conducted in Leicester in 1717. Justice Parker was the presiding magistrate, Mother Norton and her daughter the accused. All the by-then illegal acts of Witch-finding had been used on the couple. They had been put through the swimming ordeal; they had been well and truly stripped and pricked "publickly before a great number of good women." They had also, by all accounts, put up a good fight. On a number of occasions extra help had to be called to hold them down. Yet for all the confidence of the mob, the Grand Jury of the Assizes, with Justice Parker presiding, found them not guilty. In the same year and in the same town, a Jane Clark, together with her son and daughter, are said to have been tried, though many points were confused with the Norton trial, for the records are very inconclusive. In Scotland the true persecutions lasted a little longer, with the last person charged with Witchcraft, Janet Horne, being burned in 1727.

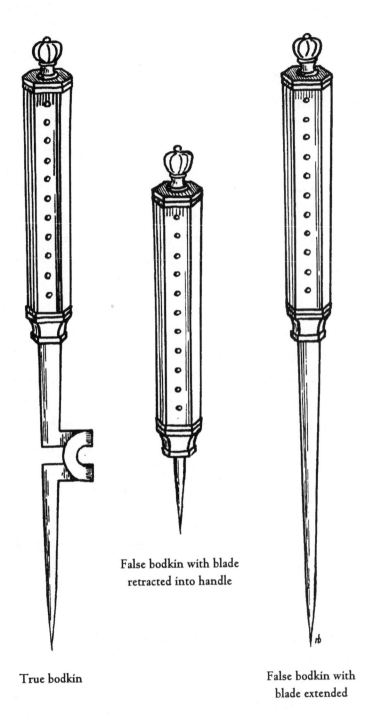

False bodkin with blade
retracted into handle

True bodkin

False bodkin with
blade extended

Types of bodkins used by witch-prickers to discover the invisible,
insensitive "devil's mark"

The Witchcraft Act of James I (James VI of Scotland), passed in England in 1604, was finally repealed in 1736. It had been virtually obsolete for forty or fifty years before that date and seemed a clear indication that Christianity had finally triumphed. It had certainly shown its strength in no uncertain manner—those it had not been able to convert, it had destroyed. Witchcraft, the Old Religion, was finally dead...or so it seemed.

6: THE LIVING DEAD

ut was the Old Religion really dead? A set of beliefs that had grown up and lasted over many thousands of years did not die that easily. Underground, in hiding, the Wica still lived. Small groups, surviving covens, individual families, kept the religion alive. Not the Witchcraft depicted by the Christians, not the Devil-worship and evil magick variety, but the Wican worship of the old gods, the communion with nature and love of all life.

In the literary field, of course, Christianity had no rivals. From the block-printing of the twelfth century through to the beginning of the twentieth century, virtually all works on the subject of Witchcraft were from the Church's point of view. Pennethorne Hughes (*Witchcraft*, Longmans Green, London, 1952) makes a very good point when he says:

> The secrets and rites of the Witches were not committed to paper...the record of Witchcraft is that set down by its enemies. It is as though, in a world conquered by the Third Reich, all Jewish tradition and history had been destroyed— together with the Bible and the Jews themselves— so that later generations knew of Jews only as portrayed by the men of Nurenberg. (In time, no doubt, skeptics would have asked whether such monsters had ever really existed at all.)

Arguments in print there certainly were, though not Old Religion versus New. In a sense the centuries of Christian propaganda had been too successful. Now no one knew quite what to believe. Richard Boulton's *Complete History of Magic, Sorcery and Witchcraft*, which appeared in 1715, accepted completely the many and various stories developed against the Witches. He believed implicitly that they flew through the air, that they changed their appearance, that they worshiped the Devil. He was stopped short three years later by the publication of Francis Hutchinson's *Historical Essay Concerning Witchcraft* which, in a very down-to-earth manner, dealt with the delusions of sick minds, acceptance of the evidence of small children, political aspects, perjurers, etc.. Boulton tried to reply to this undermining of his naïve beliefs but Hutchinson's work had hit home. On the repeal of the James I Witchcraft Act, the statute stated that there was now no such thing as Witchcraft, and to pretend to have occult powers was to face being charged with fraud!

In London, in the mid-eighteenth century, Witchcraft per se dropped from the public's mind for a while with the formation of one of the most notorious of secret societies: Sir Francis Dashwood's Friars of St. Francis of Wycombe, better known, perhaps, as the "Hellfire Club." Sir Francis who, at the age of sixteen, had been left a fortune on his father's death, formed his group from the wildest yet wealthiest, and also most intelligent, young men of his time. In 1752 he took a ruined medieval abbey, at West Wycombe, for the headquarters for himself and his twelve followers. From the outset he was bent on ridiculing religion, especially Catholicism.

Some time previously he had, as he thought, witnessed a vision of an angel. He felt immediately converted and spared no effort or expense to convert others to the Church. Later, the only other witness to the "vision"—his tutor—let out the true story of how young Dashwood, much the worse for drink, had mistaken two mating cats for devils fighting for his, Sir Francis's, soul. He had then further mistaken the tutor, in his nightshirt, for an angel dressed in white. Dashwood was mercilessly ridiculed for his period of piousness and so he felt that he had to hit back; he had to show that he really had no respect whatsoever for religion.

The ruined Medmenham Abbey was extensively remodeled and decorated for his use. Stained glass windows were installed showing himself and his twelve "apostles" in various indecent postures. Many were the frescoes: copies of Greek and Roman "indecent" paintings, together with ideas of his own. Over the entrance to the abbey was the inscription *Fay ce que voudras*— "Do what thou wilt," a motto later to be used by Aleister Crowley, who had a similar if less pretentious abbey at Cefalu, in Sicily, in 1921.

The basis of the Hellfire Club, as stated, was ridicule of religion. This took the form of Satanism, or Diabolism. Just how seriously the club members really took the Satanic side of the organization is in some doubt. That they held "services," attempted Black Masses, is certain. It seems more certain, however, that their main interest was in sex, and to this end it seemed that Sir Francis always had an ample supply of young women on hand to satisfy each and every taste.

The Old Religion, Wica, was accused of parodying the Christian mass. Why it was thought the Witches would spend their time mimicking another religion's rites when they had their own much older rituals to do was never explained. That they actually did not parody the mass is certain, yet they were persecuted for it. The Hellfire Club, on the other hand, set out to do just that, and more. Yet because of the titles and positions of its members—such as William Hogarth, the Earl of Sandwich, the Earl of Bute, Charles Churchill, Lord Melcombe, George Selwyn—nothing was done. For roughly thirty years Sir Francis held court at Medmenham. Members left, or died, and their places were taken by others. At one time Ben Franklin was a member. Eventually, with deaths and internal disagreements, the Order fell apart. On December 11, 1781, Sir Francis died.

By the mid-nineteenth century, after much discussion of whether Witches did or did not exist, popular opinion had settled for a somewhat romantic-rationalist approach. In 1831 first appeared Sir Walter Scott's *Demonology and Witchcraft* (Harper's Family Library, No. XI). This work was to become enormously popular, its main theme being the identification of the Witches and fairies with submerged races in Europe. This theme was to be examined further a hundred years after Scott by Dr. Margaret Murray. Sir David Brewster did a supplement to Scott's work in his *Letters on Natural Magic* (Harper's Family Library, No. L, 1832).

The Abbots Bromley Horn Dancers

While the people of the cities and towns enjoyed Scott and his many imitators, surviving Pagan festivities were still going on unnoticed in the countryside. In County Kerry, Ireland, at the little village of Killorglin, was held the annual August Eve Puck Fair. The King of the Fair, and indeed "Puck King of Ireland," was none other than a horned goat. The goat was treated with great pomp and ceremony, its horns and feet painted gold and garlands hung about its neck. The fair lasted for three days. Each day the goat would be treated with more and greater respect, being displayed on a platform made higher each successive day, until its actual "crowning" on the third and final day. Significantly, shortly after the crowning the goat was killed, roasted, and eaten amidst general rejoicing—an undoubted survival of the substitute Divine King.*

---

*cf. *The Divine King in England* Margaret Murray, Faber, London 1954.

Another truly Pagan festival took place, and still takes place, not far from London at Abbots Bromley. At the Winter Solstice they have there a performance of the age-old Horn Dance. Early in the morning a procession goes to the church to collect the famous reindeer horns, which are stored in a chapel. These horns weigh an average of 20 pounds each and are attached to carved wooden deer heads, in turn bound with iron to short, stout staves. The six dancers in the procession carry them in front of their faces. Also in the procession are a hobbyhorse, a fool, and a man dressed as an old woman who carries an ancient phalliform ladle. Together with a boy hitting a triangle and a musician playing an accordion, they all set off around the village boundaries, stopping at each and every farm and cottage to perform an intricate dance. It has been suggested that the Abbots Bromley Horn Dance stems from an enforcement of forest rights for the people or, going further back, an example of sympathetic magick to entice deer.

Pennethorne Hughes tells of a May Day march and dance celebrated in Wales. It was called the *Cadi*. The leading garland-bearer wore a hideously painted mask and led the thirteen dancers in singing and round dances. May Day celebrations generally are most interesting as examples of surviving Paganism. The phallic symbolism of the Maypole or Tree is generally accepted, the distribution of gifts or prizes from it emphasizing its fruit-bearing qualities. B.Z. Goldberg (*The Sacred Fire*, 1930) observes:

> Like the rod or the pole, the tree graphically rep-
> resented the lingam. But it also suggested the gen-
> erative organ functionally; standing erect, rooted
> in the ground and stretching skyward, withstand-

ing all assault of the weather, the tree emphasizes power and virility. Bedecking its branches with green leaves and bearing fruit, it was generative in no unmistakable manner. The tree was, then, a living image of the lingam.

An interesting comparison with the Maypole, in this respect, is the ancient Egyptian *Djed*-column pictured being raised at Memphis, on a relief in the tomb of Kheraf at Thebes. The Pharaoh, High Priest of Memphis, and several slaves are depicted hauling on ropes to raise the column. A very ancient symbol of Osiris, before it was identified with Ptah at Memphis, the *Djed*-column could well have originally been a tree with its branches trimmed.

Herdsmen in Sweden still follow an old practice of cutting the first bough of a mountain ash that the sun strikes on May Day morning. With this bough they will then strike the horns and flanks of their cattle, chanting: "As the sap comes to the trees, may milk come to these udders." In Pennsylvania mountain ash and witch hazel are hung over barn doors for protection from evil magick.

While Pagan festivals were still being so openly celebrated there were many more less-publicized practices going on. An important side of the Wica was a knowledge of herbs, charms, and cures. In the nineteenth century this side came very much to the fore, especially in the outlying districts. There practically every village had its Cunning Man or Wise Woman, wise in the lore, who, like the early Wica, was looked upon as a beneficent combination of family doctor and minister. They would be consulted for everything from thorn-pricks to childbirth. It was not uncommon for people to travel from the towns out to the country,

A Witch working a magickal cure on a man's foot

After Ulrich Molitor, *De Lamiis*, 1489

to consult with some of the better known ones—those such as "Cunning" Murrell of Essex, England, or old "Doc" Teare on the Isle of Man.

After Cunningman James Murrell's death in December 1860, Arthur Morrison went to his cottage, together with Murrell's son, hoping to find material for an article later to appear in *The Strand* magazine, in London. Unfortunately the younger Murrell had destroyed most of his father's records and apparatus before Morrison contacted him. What was left, however, was of great interest. There were letters asking for help from people all over the country, from well-to-do London families to local farmers and laborers. There were herbs hanging drying, in bunches, from the ceiling of the cottage. There were books which, apparently indecipherable to Morrison, contained astronomical details and charts for horoscopes. Morrell had also, it seems, made frequent use of a "magick mirror" and of various amulets.

The Ozark region of Missouri and Arkansas even today reflects the general tone of European village life in the mid to late nineteenth century. Beliefs about the auspicious times for planting crops, lucky charms, omens, and auguries abound. Love potions, water-divining, spells, charms, and exorcisms: all show a great feeling for the old Craft. Pagan beliefs and superstitions abound.

The old knowledge was not dead, and neither were the old gods. They were still being worshiped and revered, secretly but devoutly, as they had been for the past three hundred years. And the time was drawing near when, once again, the worshippers could come out of hiding and worship openly. The time was at hand.

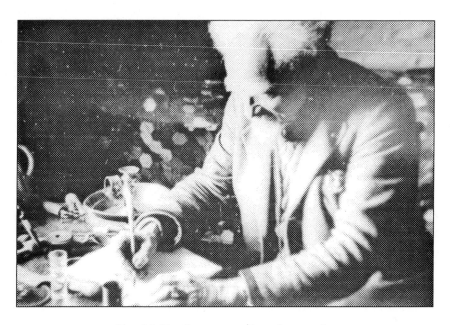

Gerald Gardner at work in his study

7: WITCHES AWAKE!

The word "anthropology" is derived from a combination of the Greek words *anthrops*, meaning "man," and *logia*, meaning "study." Anthropology, then, means "the study of Man." It was not until the 1920s that anthropology turned its studies to Witchcraft. Previous to that time the only thing approaching an anthropological approach to the subject had been Charles Godfrey Leland's book *Aradia: Gospel of the Witches of Italy*, published in 1899. At that time this study came under the rather antiquarian heading of "Folklore."

C.G. Leland was a most prolific writer who wrote, enlighteningly, on every conceivable subject from *Dainty Hints to Epicurean Smokers* through *The Algonquin Legends of New England* to *A Manual of Wood Carving*. He was a most energetic collector, also founder and first president of the Gypsy Lore Society. In 1885 Leland met a young woman named Maddelena who claimed to be a Witch. She further claimed to be a descendant of a long line of Witches. She came from the wild, wooded area of Romagna Toscana, and Leland first encountered her in the back streets of Florence. Some years later, when Leland had settled permanently in Florence, Maddelena promised to obtain for him a copy of the local Witches' book, or "Gospel" (*Vangelo*), of which he had heard rumors. The book turned out to be of great interest and, he thought, probably very old. T.C. Lethbridge feels that the *Vangelo* itself is probably no older than the Middle Ages but is conceivably based on an underlying belief far older. It is, as he remarks, somewhat warped from political propaganda. Two alternative texts are given in the *Vangelo*. In the one Diana, or Tana, is the Queen of All Witches and, as the Moon, has union with her brother Lucifer, the Sun. From this union is produced Aradia, to be the Messiah of the Witch cult. She is to teach various remunerative and ofttimes vindictive arts to an oppressed race. The other text deals with the act of creation, depicting Diana as "the first darkness." Her brother is the first light and, again, from their union comes Aradia. Leland associates Aradia—probably correctly—with Herodias.

When Leland's *Aradia* first appeared it was greeted with little of the enthusiasm that he expected. The general opinion was that he had had his leg pulled by his Italian "Witch" and that there was really no truth to any of it! That the book did not become popular is, perhaps, a good thing from the point of view of many present-day Witches, for much of what Leland published was, in fact, very close to Witchcraft as it is known and practiced in Europe today.

In 1917 an article by Dr. Margaret Alice Murray appeared in *Folklore* (Vol. 28) headed "Organizations of Witches in Great

Britain." Three years later Volume 31 of *Folklore* carried another of Dr. Murray's articles, this one titled "Witches and the Number 13." Dr. Murray was an eminent anthropologist and Assistant Professor in Egyptology at University College, London. In 1921 she published a book titled *The Witch-Cult in Western Europe*, which was a careful study of evidence provided by the contemporary reports of the Witchcraft trials. For the first time someone—a scholar of note—was looking at the subject of Witchcraft with an unbiased eye.

This was to be the first of a number of such unbiased works as more and more historians and anthropologists realized that there was, almost certainly, some basis to the theory that Murray put forward. She dared to suggest that Witchcraft was actually the survival of a pre-Christian religion. Dr. Murray had done a great deal of research, going through the legal records of the trials and contemporary pamphlets with a fine-tooth comb.

Much of the trial evidence had to be disregarded since it had been obtained under torture, but there was no question in Murray's mind that behind the Christian façade of the time was a cult which could be traced back to pre-Christian times. As she says in her introduction:

> The god, anthropomorphic or theriomorphic, was
> worshipped in well-defined rites; the organization
> was highly developed; and the ritual is analogous
> to many ancient rituals.

Together with *The Witch-Cult in Western Europe* must be considered Dr. Murray's second book on the subject, *God of the Witches* (Sampson, Low Marston, London, 1931) published ten years later. In the interim she had researched further and, whereas her first book stayed closely with the records of the Middle Ages, her second book delved back to search for the origins of the religion in pre-Christian times.

Murray's works caused great excitement on their appearance and initiated an open-minded view of the subject, a view that had been sadly lacking for many centuries. However, it was not until several years later—after World War II, in fact—that there was to be anything approaching a confirmation of her theories.

In 1949 there appeared an historical novel bearing the title *High Magic's Aid*, its author having the pseudonym "Scire." This was an enjoyable story involving ceremonial magick and Witchcraft, the Witchcraft of the very variety researched so carefully by Dr. Margaret Murray. But it was to be another five years before the author's real name appeared, and then it was on a work of non-fiction: *Witchcraft Today*. The author's name was Gerald Brousseau Gardner, and his new book was to become the answer, for millions of people, to the question, "What is Witchcraft…*really?*"

In effect, what Gardner said with his book was: "What Dr. Murray and others have suggested is correct…Witchcraft certainly *was* a religion, and in fact it still is. I know because I am a Witch!" Gardner was indeed a practicing member of one of the surviving ancient covens of the Witch cult in England. *Witchcraft Today* was to become the number one book on the list of anyone at all interested in the survival of the Craft. Regarding his earlier work (*High Magic's Aid*), Gardner wrote:

> As it is a dying cult I thought it was a pity that all the knowledge should be lost, so in the end I was permitted to write, as fiction, something of what a Witch believes in the novel *High Magic's Aid*.

This present volume (*Witchcraft Today*) has the same purpose, but deals with the subject in a factual way.

Destined to end his days known as the "Grand Old Man of British Witchcraft," Gardner had spent the whole of his life studying magickal beliefs around the world. He was born near Blundellsands, Lancashire, England, on Friday, June 13, 1884, to a family of Scottish ancestry. His father, William, was a justice of the peace and also travelled extensively for the family timber business. His mother was a member of the prestigious Browning Society and, although she produced four other boys besides Gerald, remained more interested in social life than family life. Gerald suffered greatly from asthma and, at four years of age, was sent off to Europe with an Irish nurse, Josephine McCombie, in the hopes of finding a climate that would suit him. At the age of seven, in the Canary Islands, he purchased a knife that was to be the first of a huge collection of weapons he was to accumulate on his travels.

By 1900 Gardner was in Ceylon and starting his first job on a tea plantation. While working on this and other plantations, he spent as much of his spare time as possible in the jungle, talking to the native people and studying their beliefs. He was, at about this time, visited by his parents and an American relative named Jenny Tompkins. Jenny gave him a Bible, asking him to read it carefully and adding: "I read it from cover to cover when I was your age and I have never believed a word of it since!" Gardner read it, as instructed, and reached much the same conclusion.

While he worked on a variety of plantations, tea and rubber, over the next few years, Gardner read all he could on anthropology and made copious notes on all local customs and beliefs with which he came into contact, both in Ceylon and later in Borneo. He found that he got on extremely well with a group of head-hunters, the Dyaks, and was even invited to attend some of their rituals. These, he said later, were remarkably similar to spiritualist meetings.

After a short stay with the Rajah of Sarawak, Gardner worked for a year in Malaya, where he learned a lot from an acquaintance who had studied the magick of the Malays, Saki, and Borneans. By 1925 he had passed through a variety of jobs including, as a customs patrolman, intercepting smugglers in the Indian Ocean. As a government inspector of opium establishments, he found he had a great deal of time on his hands, which he spent in studying. He particularly studied the Saki and their personal weapon, the kris, or keris—a wavy-bladed knife. By the time he wrote his first book, *Kris and Other Malay Weapons*, Gardner had become established as the world authority on this subject. He also became an authority on the ancient history of Johore, establishing that there had been an ancient Malay culture, gold coinage, and large ocean-going ships. He even succeeded in discovering four miles of earthworks, the real site of the ancient city of Singapura.

In 1934 Gardner took a trip to Saigon, in what was then French-Indochina, then went on to China itself. When finally, in 1936, he left the East to retire to England, he worked his way back via the Wellcome Archaeological Research Expedition in Palestine, at the ancient city of Lachish.

Back in England he came into contact with a number of people interested in the occult. After his years of research into various magickal beliefs, Gardner was fascinated to one day hear mention of Witchcraft in connection with his Grandfather

Gerald Gardner

Joseph's second wife, Ann. Without being able to get any details, it seemed that she had been—at least by repute—a Witch. A previous ancestress of his, Grizell Gairdener, had been burned as a Witch at Newborough, Scotland, in 1640. It was casual reference to these facts that ended with Gardner being himself initiated into a surviving Witchcraft coven near Christchurch, just a few days after the start of the Second World War.

Finding what "the Craft," Witchcraft, really was—the fact that it was not Satanism or devil-worship or the like and that it was, in fact, a very positive, nature-based religion—and the fact that it was still alive, Gardner was extraordinarily happy. So much so that he wanted to tell the world, tell everyone how wrong they had been. But, of course, he was not allowed to do so. He was told that the only way the Craft had kept going was by meeting secretly and remaining completely underground. However, the exuberant Gardner finally persuaded his coven, and in particular his High Priestess, "Old Dorothy," to permit him to write something of the truth in the form of a novel. This was to be *High Magick's Aid*, written under his Witch name, Scire.

In 1950 Gardner finally found the ideal place to house his enormous collection of magickal apparatus and of ancient and primitive weapons. It was an old mill, mentioned in court records of 1611 and historically associated with Witches, on the Isle of Man (in the middle of the Irish Sea), near Castletown. The story is told that after the mill was gutted by fire in the last century the ruins became the dancing ground of the local Arbory Witches. In 1952 Gardner purchased it from Cecil Williamson, who had been using it as his headquarters for the Witchcraft Research Association. Here Gardner settled, purchasing a stone-built, oak-beamed, seventeenth-century cottage on Castletown's High Street, and opened the world's first Museum of Magic and Witchcraft at the old mill. With the death of his original priestess, Gardner finally managed to convince his coven that it would be good for the Craft if a factual book were done to explain their beliefs and practices. So, *Witchcraft Today* was published, to be followed in

1959 by a complementary volume, *The Meaning of Witchcraft.* And, as Gardner foresaw, these two books did magnificent work in helping correct many of the misconceptions about Witchcraft. With the books and his museum, which had become a center of study for students of the subject, Gardner himself became the unofficial leader of European Witchcraft, more learned in the laws and history of the Craft than many High Priestesses.

It had taken a lot of courage to be the first to stand up and admit to being a Witch. For a long time Gardner suffered the irritation of broken windows, anonymous letters and telephone calls, and the rest of the senseless bigotry. But 1951 had seen the repeal of the Witchcraft Act of 1735, Witches were now free to come out of hiding and worship openly—if they had the courage. Possibly in recognition of Gardner's courage, and distinguished work, in 1960 he received the cachet of an invitation to a reception at Buckingham Palace.

The work of Murray and Gardner* was bearing fruit. This is a century of intelligence. Intelligence to think for oneself, to ask questions, to investigate. By 1955 Professor Varagnac, in Paris University, was giving lectures on Witchcraft based on Murray's and Gardner's works. In 1959 Dr. Serge Hutin wrote (*Ecole Pratique des Lautes Etudes Sciences Religieuses*):

---

*Gardner did not do all of his literary work alone. He was hampered by being dyslexic, and eventually much of the writing was done by Doreen Valiente, who had been initiated by Gardner in 1953. There has been much controversy, since Gardner's death in 1964, as to how much of the Book of Shadows (the book containing all the coven's rituals, laws, etc.) was genuinely dated from ancient times. Aidan A. Kelly's book *Crafting the Art of Magic* (Llewellyn, St. Paul, 1991) investigates this in some depth, as do several of Doreen Valiente's own books

> The most qualified specialist in this field [Witch-
> craft], Dr. Gerald Gardner of the Isle of Man,
> relies strongly on these survivals (of the ancient
> cult), which contain nothing dangerous to public
> order.

In New York in 1964 the New School for Social Research carried a course entitled "Witchcraft, Magic, and Sorcery," taught by
the late Dr. Joseph Kaster (at which this author appeared a number of times as a guest lecturer). A Reuter report from Farnham,
England, dated March 3, 1966, reads: "An adult education centre
here reported today that 50 applications have been received for
enrollment in a three-day course in Witchcraft."

The interest in the subject of Witchcraft, *as a religion*, is
tremendous. Gardner initially wrote of the Craft as a "dying
cult," but in later years he had to revise his thinking. Since the
persecutions, with covens going into hiding, contact has been
lost between one group and the next. Today more and more
covens are cautiously re-emerging from hiding, getting into contact with one another again. It was a sad loss to Witchcraft, and
to anthropology, when on February 12, 1964, Gerald Gardner
died at sea, on his way home from a winter vacation in Lebanon.
Whatever else may be said about Gerald Gardner, he did more
than anyone to establish a return to the old ways, to allow people to once more make contact with the Old Religion.

8: THE RITUALS OF WITCHCRAFT

It has been said, repeatedly, that Witchcraft is a religion. What exactly is meant by that? How do Witches worship and where? What form does the worship take?

First of all Witchcraft is a religion, as any other religion, in that a group of people come together at certain times of the year to worship, in their own particular way, the gods in whom they believe. The gods "in whom they believe" are the gods of nature; they are based in the ancient God of hunting and the Goddess of fertility of early humankind's beliefs. It would be wrong to say— as some have—that there is an unbroken line of worshippers from Paleolithic times through to the present. No. Obviously different countries, and even different areas of one country, have developed in different ways over the millennia. What we see as Witchcraft in recent times is the way those religious beliefs have developed throughout Western Europe and, for the sake of this present writing, in Britain and, later, America specifically.

A group of Witches is termed a *coven*. The origin of the word is uncertain but it probably comes from the word "convene." It was first mentioned by one of the Auldearn Witches, Isobel Gowdie, in 1662 when, at her trial, she spoke of there being "thirteen persons in each coven." In fact it is this author's belief that covens were a relatively recent system, probably inspired by the pressure of the persecutions. Prior to that time it was not uncommon for whole villages to gather together to celebrate the festivals—the seed planting, the pruning, the harvesting, and so on. Similarly it was not uncommon for individuals, or individual families, to worship, supplicate, or give thanks to the gods, on their own property and away from others. But with the Witch hunts of the persecutions, the "hard core," as it were, of the Old Religion's followers needed to band together. This, it is felt, led to the formation of covens.

Perhaps from Isobel Gowdie's statement the belief has built up that a coven of Witches *must* be made up of thirteen people. This is not true. There can actually be any number of Witches that will comfortably fit into the meeting place. That meeting place is a marked circle, frequently of about nine feet diameter. It can readily be seen, therefore, that there would be a maximum number and that could approach about a dozen. If one thinks in terms of couples, then six couples together with a Priestess would give a traditional thirteen, but this is by no means manda-tory. In a really large circle you could fit as many as a hundred Witches if you wanted to. Conversely, just two Witches might meet together in a small circle. Either would be termed a coven, if that was how they regularly met.

Goddess of the Witches

The religion is a polytheistic one, though there are two main deities: the Horned God and the Goddess. These two, in fact, are the only ones with names. The other gods—presumably carry-overs from those of early humankind's animistic conceptions—are simply referred to as "the Mighty Ones" or just as "the Gods." One might see a parallel with the Roman Catholic Saints.

The Goddess, as has been seen, is a Goddess of birth and rebirth and the God one of hunting and nature generally. He is also referred to as "the god of death and all that comes after." Within the coven these two deities are represented by a Priest and Priestess. In many traditions,* since the Goddess, as a bearer of life, is perceived as being of somewhat greater importance than the God, so the Priestess is regarded as slightly more important than the Priest. For example, in many traditions a meeting can take place with the Priestess present but the Priest absent but cannot take place with the Priest and no Priestess.

The coven meets at a place known as the *covenstead*, which, these days, is usually the home of the Priestess. In the old days the group would meet out in the open, in a field or a clearing in the woods. Being a nature-based religion, it seemed appropriate to meet close to the earth. But with the pressures of the growing persecutions, meetings were restricted to inside isolated cottages or, at best, a deserted clearing in the woods far from the nearest village or town, somewhere where the group would not be discovered.

If there were several covens within a region there had to be a way to break them down into specific areas so that one coven, or Priestess, would not "step on the toes" of another. It was

---

*As in Christianity there is found a wide variety of denominations, so in Witchcraft. These denominations, or traditions, include Keltic, Saxon, Gardnerian, Scottish, Welsh, Alexandrian, Dianic, and many more.

Wican altar, Gardnerian tradition

therefore stipulated that the covendom of any one Priestess would extend outward for one league (about three miles) in all directions from the covenstead. The closest one covenstead could be to another, therefore, would be six miles. These days, with covens so widely scattered, not too much attention need be paid to the three mile radii.

Being a religion very close to nature, many traditions insist that Witches come together in pairs, equal numbers of male and female. As in nature there is always found both male and female, so with the gods and so with the worshippers. Yet there are traditions today who do not follow this belief. There are groups who, for example, focus on the Goddess even to the exclusion of the God. Similarly there are a few who focus on the God to the exclusion of the Goddess. To many, such extremes seem at variance with the whole concept of the Old Religion; as a religion of nature it depends on balance between the two. Indeed, it was the New Religion's emphasis on the male deity, to the total exclusion of the female, that lost them the conversion of the majority of Old Religion followers.

Although many Pagan peoples built temples to their gods, the Wica generally did not. They felt closer to their gods by meeting out in the open. Yet a consecrated area was needed to enclose the worshippers. What easier way than to simply draw a large circle around the people? And that is what was done. A circle is inscribed on the ground (or drawn on the floor of a building), and it is then duly consecrated by the Priest or Priestess. The coven's circle can be of any size, depending on the number of participants, though many traditions specify one of nine feet diameter, to limit the size of the group. (Looking at the working of "magick," it can be seen that there is a good reason to so limit the maximum size.)

In the center of the circle is the altar. Again, in the "old days," the altar might well have been a large rock or a tree stump. The wheel symbolism is found a lot in Wica and here it can be seen with the altar—the central, most important, feature—as the hub of the "wheel" of the circle. On the altar are placed the various instruments used in the rituals.

Like the old religions of ancient Greece and Rome, the Craft is what would be termed a "mystery religion." One cannot just become a Witch or be born a Witch, any more than, for example, one is born a Roman Catholic. One can be born into a Roman Catholic family, yes. But to actually become a member of the Church it is necessary to go through a number of rituals such as baptism, confirmation, communion, etc. In the same way, one can be born into a Witch family yet still not be a Witch until initiated into the religion.

Gerald Gardner, in *Witchcraft Today*, deals extensively with the Villa of Mysteries: the home of the Dionysian mysteries, situated on the Street of Tombs at Pompeii, Italy. This was where virtually everyone in the country would go to be initiated. Yet though so many went through it—including the slaves—very little is known of what went on there, other than what can be gathered from study of the frescoes which decorate the walls of the initiation room. These almost-life-size frescoes depict a woman going through the initiation into the Orphic mystery. They are of special interest to a Witch since many points can be recognized as almost identical to a Craft initiation.

The essence of the mystery is the death and resurrection of the deity, termed the *palingenesis*. In the initiation, the neophyte identifies with the deity and goes through a symbolical death and rebirth. This death and rebirth is common among many primitive peoples even today, as part of initiation and puberty ceremonies. They, however, do not think of the death as symbolic—many of them believe that they will quite literally be killed. All such ceremonies involve a revelation of a secret and sacred knowledge. In the Congo, for instance, initiates are called *nganga*, "the knowing ones," while the non-initiated are the *vanga*, "unenlightened."*

As Mircea Eliade says in his introduction to *Birth and Rebirth* (Harper, New York, 1958):

> The term initiation in the most general sense denotes a body of rites and oral teachings whose purpose is to produce a decisive alteration in the religious and social status of the person being initiated.

---

*cf. *The Book of African Divination* Raymond Buckland and Kathleen Binger, Inner Traditions Int'l, Vermont, 1992.

In philosophical terms, initiation is equivalent to a basic change in existential condition; the novice emerges from his ordeal endowed with a totally different being from that which he possessed before his initiation; he has become *another*.

That he has become "another" is emphasized in Witchcraft by the taking of a new name. Gardner's pseudonym for his book *High Magic's Aid* was "Scire," which was also his Craft name. It is worth noting that a newly elected pope will take a new name, as will a nun when she takes her vows.

Death and rebirth, as encountered in various primitive societies, can be extremely interesting. The symbolical death varies from scourging to actual mutilation, circumcision being the most common. The ceremonies are treated with the utmost seriousness and are prepared for way in advance with the isolating of the neophytes. The ceremony itself is led by the tribal chief or the shaman, who frequently wears a mask representing the tribe's totemic ancestor. The rite is witnessed by the fathers and elder brothers of the neophytes.

Frequently the neophytes are blindfolded and bound. They are told that the gods, or the ancestral spirits, will be coming to judge them, to kill them, and to take them away. At this point, in many widely separated places around the world, the bull-roarer or *rhombus* is brought into play. This is a piece of wood or bone which, on being whirled around on the end of a long piece of cord, produces a strange, windy, roaring sound. It was, and is, used by the Apache Indians, the ancient Greeks, the Australian Aboriginals, Africans, Maoris, and many others. To a frightened, blindfolded initiate, the sound could well be taken for that of approaching supernatural beings.

Interspersed with the "frightening" and the "death," and other necessary parts of the initiation, are teachings of the tribal myths and lores. Often a "monster" is featured in the primitive rites, which swallows the neophyte only to "give birth" or disgorge him at a later stage. In some tribes the rebirth is symbolized by the initiate crawling through between the legs of the gathered women of the tribe. After initiation, the catharsis complete, the return to the village is as a newborn child, and often his "previous" mother may not even be recognized. Frequently, too, the initiate has difficulty walking, speaking, eating; he must learn these things all over again. He has truly been reborn.

The Wica initiation is perhaps not as emotionally profound as some primitive ones, but it does contain all the ingredients. It might be regarded as roughly halfway between those primitive rites and the highly stylized, esoteric mysteries of such organizations as the Freemasons. The difference in approach yet similarity of ideas between these two can be seen in the opening exchange between Wican High Priestess and initiate on the one hand and the Senior Steward, Senior Deacon, Master, and initiate on the other.

Dealing with Masonic initiation first, the lodge room has an altar in the center on which is found a square, compass and Bible. There are three lighted tapers around. The initiate, or "candidate," is prepared by removing his coat, trousers, shoes, and socks and ensuring that he has nothing made of metal with him. The Senior Steward further prepares him by giving him another pair of pants, a slipper for his right foot only, and a blindfold. His left arm is put through the front of his shirt so that his left breast is exposed. Around his neck is tied a blue silk rope, or "cable-tow," and he is then ready to proceed. The candidate is caused to knock three times on the lodge door, causing the Senior Deacon inside to inform the Master that there is "an alarm." However, the Senior Steward reassures all by saying: "A poor blind candidate, who is desirous of being brought from darkness to light and receiving a part of the lights, rights, and benefits of this worshipful lodge, erected to God and dedicated to the Holy Saint John, as many a brother and fellow has done before him."

A number of questions and answers are then relayed back and forth between the candidate and the Senior Deacon, with the Senior Steward answering most of them for the candidate. Then, when the candidate finally enters the lodge proper, the Senior Deacon takes up the compass, presses the point to the candidate's left breast, and says: "My friend, it is the will and pleasure of the Worshipful Master that I receive you into this lodge of Entered Apprentices in due and ancient form. I receive you on the point of a sharp instrument at your naked left breast, which is to show that, as this is an instrument of torture to the flesh, so should the remembrance thereof be to your conscience, should you ever attempt to reveal the secrets of Masonry unlawfully." This part of the initiation is called the "Shock of Entrance."

The candidate goes on to receive instruction and introduction to the lodge officers, to swear an oath, kiss the Bible, "receive light," receive the secret work of this degree (viz., the symbolism of the articles on the altar, the name of the grip—Boaz), to receive his white lambskin apron, and to be presented with "the working tools of an Entered Apprentice."

Now let's look at the initiation into the Gardnerian branch of Wica—that denomination founded by Gerald Gardner. It is a very popular tradition on both sides of the Atlantic and typical of many such Craft initiations.

The Wica initiate is prepared very simply—he is stripped naked. In the case of a woman, a necklace would be worn—the Wican symbol of rebirth—but nothing else. A man is initiated by the Priestess of the coven and a woman by the Priest of the coven; again, the balance of male/female being respected.

On entering the temple and stopping outside the circle marked on the floor, the Initiate is confronted by a very stern-faced woman, the Priestess, with raised sword pointing at him, who asks if he has the courage to go through with the rite. On being assured that he does, she will warn: "For I say, verily, it were better to rush on this weapon and perish than to make the attempt with fear in thy heart." Nothing daunted, the Initiate will exchange passwords with the Priestess who, being satisfied that all is well, will lower the sword. She will then come out of the Circle to the Initiate. There she will bind him and blindfold him and then lead him into the Circle, imparting the most important password to him. This part of the initiation is called "The Ordeal." It is followed by the Oath of Secrecy and a re-enactment of the *palingenesis* plus the imparting of certain secrets (*viz.* the symbolism and use of the "working tools" on the altar and the names of the gods) and the receipt of his own personal tool. There is no repudiation of a previous religion required. There are no goat's buttocks to kiss or crosses to be spat upon and trampled underfoot!

The Oath of Secrecy is given, line by line, by the Priestess and the Initiate repeats it. Once taken the blindfold can be removed. In Freemasonry's oath there is a phrase: "To all this (the oath of the First Degree) I most solemnly and sincerely promise and swear with a due and steadfast resolution to keep and perform the same, without the least equivocation, mental reservation, or secret evasion in me whatsoever, binding myself under no less penalty than that of having my throat cut from ear to ear, my tongue torn out by its roots, and my body buried in the rough sands of the sea, a cabletow length from shore, where the tide ebbs and flows twice in twenty-four hours, should I ever, knowingly or wittingly, violate or transgress this, my Entered Appentice's obligation . . ." In Freemasonry this is a purely symbolic penalty, on a par with "cross my heart and hope to die." Although every Mason once swore this oath and bound himself under this penalty, no one ever agreed to *carry out* the penalty on anyone else. Those who sought to reveal the secrets of the ancient Pagan mysteries were often done away with, but, despite rumors and slanders to the contrary, no Freemason has ever actually had to suffer the penalties of his obligations in any literal sense. If the penalties were actually carried out by some Masonic goon squad or by some mysterious man in black following the guilty party through the streets seeking vengeance, there would have been quite a blood bath over the last three hundred years: the "secrets of Masonry" have been revealed more often than the details of the love lives of British royalty! The elements of Masonic ritual as presented here were "revealed" in the first edition of this book in 1971, yet the author's throat and tongue are intact, as are the same anatomical parts of the author of the book that provided him with this information. Nevertheless, the Grand Lodges of many states have bowed to pressure from Fundamentalist Christian groups and have removed the "penalty of obligation" from all oaths.

In 1826, a Captain Morgan of Batavia, New York, disappeared after publishing some Masonic rituals. It was rumored that he had been kidnapped and cruelly murdered for daring to

publish the secrets of the Masons. Masonic apologists have
pointed out that there is no evidence for this murder that would
stand up in a court of law, that Morgan was the town drunk and
a ne'er-do-well who published the rituals as an act of revenge for
being expelled from a lodge for his behavior, and that it was far
more likely that some leading citizens of the town simply paid
him to get out of their hair and move to Canada. In any event,
the Morgan affair set off a wave of anti-Masonry that dominated
politics for years to come and almost destroyed the fraternity in
the United States.

No Freemason has ever been burned at the stake—unless
you count the Knights Templar—but there are certain resem-
blances in America in 1990 between Witch-hunting and Mason
baiting, as a recent Southern Baptist Convention will attest.

Be that as it may, in Witchcraft, there are no such dire
threats, symbolic or otherwise. No horrible curse hangs over
your head. Yet seldom, if ever, has the oath been broken.

In *Crafting the Art of Magic*, Aidan Kelly dwells extensively on
Gerald Gardner's perhaps unhealthy fascination with scourging.
Almost laughably, Kelly implies that virtually all men of Gardner's generation—or all who attended English "public" schools,
at least—became sexual deviates through suffering corporal punishment as part of the British school system! Apart from the
implausibility of this premise (Kelly seems to have been unduly
influenced by Ian Gibson's *The English Vice: Beating, Sex and
Shame in Victorian England and After*), he apparently ignores the
fact that Gardner was given his governess, Josephine "Com"
McCombie, at the age of four. Shortly thereafter the two left England to travel the world, Gerald therefore spending little time in
an English school. Gardner's predilection with scourging is not

in question, but Kelly seems to have overlooked a more probable source for its inclusion in Gardnerian ritual. That source would be the frescoes of the Villa of Mysteries at Pompeii. As mentioned above, from Gardner's *Witchcraft Today*, we know that he was well acquainted with the initiation room there. One of the scenes depicted shows the initiate being scourged. This was not uncommon as a symbolic ritual "death" and, as has been shown, this is a universal motif; an essential part of *palingenesis*. That Gardner somewhat overdoes this scourging in his rituals is acknowledged.*

Different traditions of Wica have different initiations, but all contain these same basic ingredients: a challenge, oath, imparting of knowledge, symbolical death and rebirth.

Mention was made earlier of the early followers of the Old Religion sometimes practicing by themselves or alone with their families. These solitary Wicans would do what amounted to a self-initiation. They would ritually dedicate themselves to the old gods and their ways. In *Buckland's Complete Book of Witchcraft* (Llewellyn, St. Paul, 1986) there is given, in full, such a self-dedication ritual, together with a coven initiation.

A child may be taken into the Craft, though this would be the child of a couple already in the coven. The age at which the child would be initiated would actually depend upon that particular child, its understanding and feelings. Many are brought in at about six or seven years of age. The ritual is exactly the same as for an adult with one exception—the Oath of Secrecy (where there is such an oath) is taken by the parent on the child's behalf.

---

*In the oral teachings received by the author, on his initiation into Gardnerian Wica in 1963, it was stressed that any scourging was "*not to hurt*," but purely symbolic.

At a later age—about the age of puberty—the child will go through the ceremony again and this time take the oath on its own behalf. It can be seen that there is here a parallel with the baptism and later confirmation found in many denominations of Christianity, though it might be pointed out that there is probably far less pressure brought to bear on a Wican child than its Christian counterpart. The child will only go through the later ritual, and remain in the Craft, if it sincerely wishes to do so at that time/age. If, at that time, he or she wishes to leave the Craft, then there are no barriers put up to stop that. Indeed, anyone may leave at any time. Similarly, they may rejoin later, if they so desire.

That the names of the gods are secret to the initiates is important. The Druidic and Jewish beliefs have already been mentioned in this respect. It stems from a belief that to know a person's name is to have a hold—a power—over them, for to know the name is to be able to conjure with it. Sir James Frazer (*The Golden Bough*, Macmillan, 1922) tells the story of Isis obtaining the secret name of Ra, the great Egyptian sun god, so that she might use it to make herself a goddess. Isis lay in wait till she saw Ra pass by. As he passed he spat upon the earth. Isis fashioned a serpent from the spittle of Ra and the earth on which it fell, and laid it in his path so that the next time he came by it bit him. Ra cried out for help from "the children of the gods with healing words and understanding lips, whose power reacheth to heaven…And Isis came with her craft, whose mouth is full of the breath of life, whose spells chase pain away, whose words maketh the dead to live." Ra told her how he had been stung while out walking and Isis said, "Tell me thy name, divine Father, for the man shall live who is called by this name." Ra told her many of the names by which he was known, all the time growing weaker. Isis, however, refused to heal him, repeating, "That was not thy name that thou speakest unto me. Oh tell it me, that the poison may depart; for he shall live whose name is named." Finally Ra gave Isis his true name and she caused the poison to flow away; and she became "the queen of the gods, she who knows Ra and his true name."

In Borneo the Dyaks believe very strongly in the name of power. Mothers will not call their children home after dark by the child's true name. They believe that if they did then evil spirits might hear the name and then call the children themselves. The mothers must therefore call their offspring by a "nickname." Disclosing the names even of Priests in ancient Greece was punishable by law. Frazer mentions an overly communicable Roman, Valerius Soranus, who revealed the name of Rome's guardian deity and, it seems, was subsequently executed.

The binding, which is invariably found in initiatory rites as part of the death and rebirth cycle, is especially interesting when the Paleolithic practice of trussing a corpse is borne in mind. The skeleton of Chancelade, Dordogne, France, is of an old man covered in red ochre and trussed up so tightly that he occupies a space little more than two feet long by sixteen inches wide. At La Ferraissie was found a woman doubled up in a similar fashion. Such figures have been found from the Mousterian period through the Magdalenian period. Obviously they were bound at death, and before *rigor mortis* set in. Almost equally obviously they were bound in preparation for their rebirth for, as in the Wican initiation, the binding and blindfolding symbolizes the darkness and restriction of the womb prior to birth.

There are thirty-three degrees of advancement in Scottish Rite Freemasonry. Thirty-two of these can be passed through

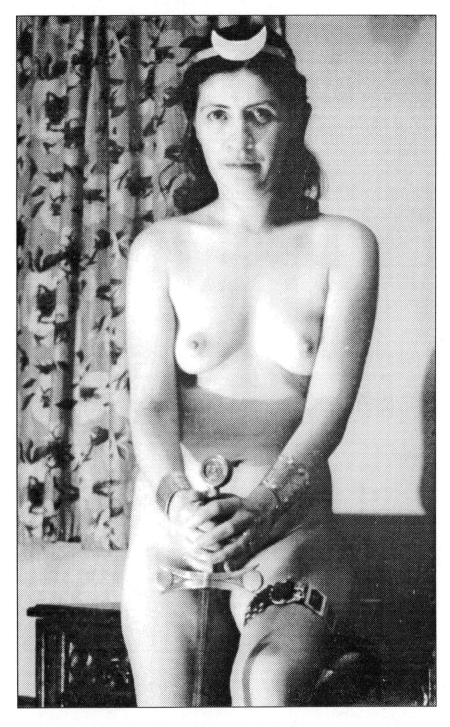

Gerald Gardner's High Priestess, the Lady Olwen, Witch Queen

almost as quickly as one can read them. (The thirty-third is honorary, a degree of recognition for service to the fraternity.) In many traditions of Wica there also exists a degree system. Most of these—Gardnerian again a good example—have three degrees only, as does the basic "Blue Lodge" Masonry exclusive of the "advanced" degrees of the Scottish Rite or York Rite. In his *Discoverie of Witchcraft* (Book III, London 1584) Reginald Scot refers to a Witch going through three "admission ceremonies."

The initiation itself is, of course, the First Degree. To take the Second Degree, a Witch must have been in the Craft for at least "a year and a day."* A similar minimum time must pass between the Second and Third degrees. (And, incidentally, the same amount of time must pass between an applicant first making contact with a coven and the date of his or her initiation.) However, a Witch is not automatically promoted but must show him or herself worthy of advancement. Many Wicans do not progress beyond the First Degree, being quite content simply to be a part of the group, without looking for any responsibility. The coven leader alone is the one who decides when, and if, a coven member is ready for the next degree.

Although one Witch talking with a stranger could tell whether or not that person was also in the Craft, there is no actual mark of identification of a regular Witch. A Priest or Priestess does have a "badge of rank," in the form of a bracelet. For a Priestess, this is a wide, flat silver bracelet with various signs and symbols engraved on it. Silver, of course, is regarded as the metal of the Moon. Since the Goddess has a close affinity

---

*This unusual period of time dates from when the calendar year went from Samhain to Samhain with one "non-day" between the 364-day years. "A year and a day," then, would encompass all of our 365-day year.

with the Moon, then silver would seem the appropriate metal for the Priestess. Similarly gold, the metal of the sun (or brass), is the metal of the bracelet worn by the Priest. This has different symbols on it from those on the Priestess's.

In traditions with a degree system, the coven Priestess is usually referred to as the *High* Priestess (and the Priest as the High Priest). In such systems, part of the duties of a Second Degree Witch is to learn the ritual duties of the Priestess and, under supervision, sometimes to carry them out. One such female is often chosen and referred to as the Maiden of the coven. These Second Degree Witches would not be allowed to perform initiations, for example, and various other rites, but generally could run the coven if necessary.

Today many Witches—and many who aren't actually initiated but have a great affinity for the Old Religion—will wear a pentagram (see below) as a symbol of the Craft. There is nothing official about this, and just because someone wears such a symbol is no guarantee that they are in the Craft.

There is another position—rather than a degree, *per se*—which may be held by some High Priestesses. This is the position of Witch Queen, or Queen of the Sabbat. When a Witch reaches the Third Degree, he or she is regarded as one of the Elders of the coven and their advice is sought on important matters affecting the group. These days, however, when someone reaches Third, they are encouraged to break away and form a new coven, to help spread the Old Religion again and get it back on its feet. If this happens—if a new coven is formed—then the High Priestess of the original coven becomes a Witch Queen, ruling over both her own coven and keeping an experienced eye on the new coven. In this way, over a period of years, one High Priestess could well become a Witch Queen with a number of covens under her, all having sprung from the original mother coven. Although she rules the new covens in name, she would never actually interfere with the new High Priestess's running of her coven unless she saw things were definitely going wrong. She is there more to give help and advice when needed. In this way everyone in the Craft has someone to turn to if necessary: the Witch to his or her High Priestess, the High Priestess to her Queen, and the Queen to *her* Queen. By virtue of being the High Priest to a High Priestess who has become a Witch Queen, the male coven leader becomes known as a *Magus*. This, however, is a purely gratuitous title.

It can be seen, then, that there are a number of Witch Queens. Yet there is no one "Queen of all Witches" (or Witch King, for that matter), despite occasional claims to the contrary. Covens are basically autonomous, so there is no one leader, no equivalent of the Roman Catholic Pope or the Church of England's Archbishop of Canterbury. Anyone claiming such a position is, quite bluntly, a fraud.

While on the subject of titles, it is interesting to see how some have rather got out of hand in recent years. It always was that the High Priestess alone would be known to her coveners as the Lady So-and-so; let's use the name "Rowena" for the sake of example. So as a coven member I would address my Priestess as "Lady Rowena" or simply "my lady." A female Witch of the Second Degree, performing ritual duties, would similarly be addressed, during the circle where she was officiating. Outside the ritual circle, the "lady" title would only be used when referring to the High Priestess. On rare ritual occasions the High Priest might be addressed with the prefix "lord," but very seldom. *All* other Witches would be known simply by their Craft names, with no title of any sort. But today it

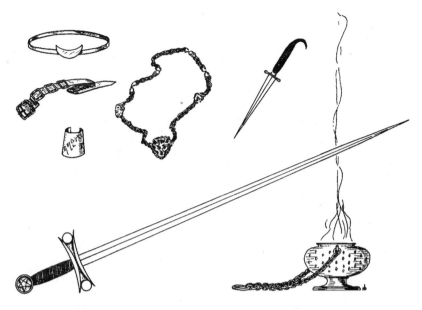

A Witch Queen's *bigghes* (jewels)—crown, garter, bracelet, and
necklace—together with athame, coven sword, and censer

seems that every other Witch is calling herself or himself "Lady
This" and "Lord That," not even restricting it to the circle, but
using it in all walks of life. It seems there are "too many chiefs and
not enough indians"! Perhaps the height of frivolity was achieved, a
few years ago, when a well-known "public" Witch adopted the title
Dame! A dame is the female equivalent of a knight and, delightful as
this particular lady was, there was no way she had ever been
dubbed by Her Majesty the Queen, and there is certainly no such
title as "dame" in Witchcraft.

The word "Witch" is used equally by both male and female
Wicans. "Warlock" is never used within the Craft. That comes
from an old Scottish word, *warloga*, meaning "deceiver" or "trai-
tor" and was applied to anyone who, during the persecutions,
gave away the names of other coven members.

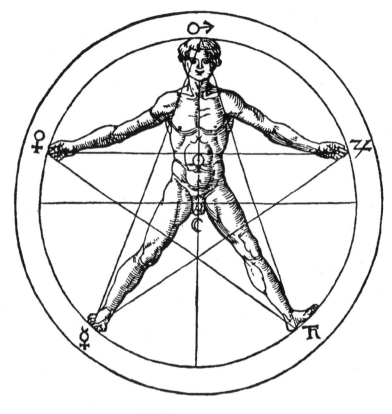

Pentagram

A Witch Queen, or Queen of the Sabbat, wears two things to show her rank. They are a silver crown, made up of a band of silver with a crescent moon at the front, and a garter. The garter is of green leather (traditionally snakeskin) backed with blue silk. On it there is one large, silver buckle, to represent the mother coven, plus other smaller silver buckles for each of the covens that have sprung from the original. This garter is worn on the left leg, just above the knee. The complete "set" of Witch's jewels—necklace, bracelet, crown, and garter—is known as the Witch Queen's *bigghes* (or *beighes*).

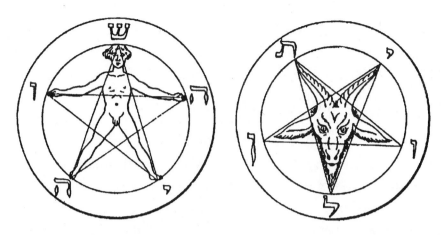

Upright and Inverted Pentagrams

In connection with the garter, Dr. Margaret Murray unearthed a fascinating tale. The usual story concerning England's King Edward III's formation of the Order of the Garter—the highest and most ancient order of knighthood in Great Britain—is that the Countess of Salisbury dropped her garter while dancing with the king. The king restored it to her, after first putting it around his own leg with the words *Honi soit qui mal y pense* ("Shame be to him who thinks evil of it"). The date for the foundation of the Order, as given by Froisant, is 1344 (other authorities assign it to 1350). As Murray points out (*God of the Witches* 1931), it took more than a dropped garter to embarrass a woman—even a lady—of the fourteenth century. This garter was obviously a ritual one, signifying that its owner was a leader of the non-Christian population. To drop that, before the many high dignitaries of the Church who were present, could certainly have caused real embarrassment. Edward's action, therefore, was very smart thinking, for in placing the garter on his own leg he not only saved face for the countess but also, in effect, proclaimed himself willing to be a leader of the

Pagan population of England as well as the Christian. This was an adroit move considering the high proportion of his subjects who were still Pagan at that time. Murray is mystified by Edward's words but, if considered as referring to *the Old Religion itself*, rather than the action or the garter, then they make admirable sense. Edward then went on to form the Order of the Garter with twenty-four knights. With himself and the Prince of Wales that was a total of twenty-six, or twice the traditional thirteen of a coven. As Chief of the Order, the king wore a blue velvet mantle powdered over with one hundred sixty-eight miniature garters. Together with the one on his leg, that made one hundred sixty-nine, or thirteen times thirteen. Significant?

To return to the jewelry. The average Witch does not wear any "official" jewelry, other than the fact that a necklace may be worn in the circle, as a symbol of the circle of rebirth. But today it seems many, if not most, Wicans want to quietly proclaim their beliefs with some symbolic jewelry—pendant necklaces and/or rings. I say "quietly"...there are those who so bedeck themselves they are literally *shouting* to the world, "I am a Witch!" Frequently these might be suspect—i.e., not actually Wicans at all, just "wannabees"!

One of the most popular symbols for jewelry is the pentagram, or five-pointed star. It is the European equivalent of the Egyptian *ankh*, in that it symbolizes the life force. Many of the old books of magick show a figure of a man or woman, standing with arms raised sideways and legs spread apart, with a five-pointed star superimposed on top of the figure. It is, then, a very positive, life-giving symbol. Unfortunately low budget movies have proclaimed it a "mark of the Devil"! Certainly many Satanists use the *inverted* (i.e., single point down and two points up) pentagram—often superimposed over a goat's head or the head of the Devil—as their symbol. The Wican/magickal one has the single point at the top.

Actually the inverted pentagram can also be found in Witch-craft. For example, it is the symbol of the Second Degree in some traditions. But this does not mean that Wica is in any way asso-ciated with Satanism; it is not. It just means that symbols are exactly that: symbols. It is not what they are; it is how they are used and what they mean to the people who use them.

9: "And Ye Shall Be Naked in Your Rites"

Mention has been made of the Wican belief in reincarnation. This is, in fact, one of the main tenets of the religion. It is a belief that we go through a number of lives and that each incarnation will be, in some way, better than the previous one; there is only progression, no regression. One could draw the parallel of a child going through the grades in a school. In each grade there is a certain amount of work, of learning, to be accomplished. Once it is done then the individual is free to take a short break then go on to the next grade, where there are more things to be learned and experienced.

Along with this belief goes another: in retribution in the present life. It is thought that whatever is done returns threefold. If good is done then good will return threefold, *in this lifetime.*

Conversely, if evil is done, then that too will return threefold, in this lifetime. There is, then, no inducement for a Witch to do evil, in any form whatsoever. This is emphasized in the one law of Witchcraft: **An it harm none, do what thou wilt.** (*An* is the Old English form of "if.") In other words, you may do anything you like…just so long as it harms no one. And that "no one" includes yourself, of course. The Witchcraft philosophy could therefore be summed up with the old expression, "Do unto others as you would have others do unto you."

It is thought that, at death, all go to the same place, known in Wica as the Summerland (similarly named by Spiritualists). There is no separate "Heaven" and "Hell," no "Judgement Day," no "Purgatory," no "Eternal Damnation"! *All* go to the Summerland, which is ruled over by the Horned God of Death and What Comes After. There is found rest and peace. One grows young again to eventually be reborn, through the agencies of the Goddess, into the next incarnation. It is the hope of every Witch to be reborn among the same people who were known in the previous life. Not all Witches can remember their past lives, though many do.

That many Witches work naked, or *skyclad* as they call it ("clad only by the sky"), is perhaps one reason their enemies claim there are wild sex orgies at their meetings! But that is a fallacy. As one Witch put it, recently: "By the time we're through with the rituals we're too darn *tired* for any orgies, even if we thought of them!" Another point is that in a nine-foot circle, with an altar in the center, there just isn't any room for half a dozen copulating couples!

The majority of covens in Europe work skyclad, but in the United States, perhaps surprisingly, most traditions seem to opt for wearing robes. In a few traditions the coveners wear robes for

Departure for the Sabbat
Engraving by Queverdo, 18th century, France

the religious rituals but will drop them, and be skyclad, for the working of magick. In my book *Buckland's Complete Book of Witchcraft* (Llewellyn, 1986), I said:

> In a recent discussion on Witchcraft, the question came up 'What proof is there that Witches always worked naked? *Is* this tradition or is it a recent innovation?'

There are certainly many early illustrations of naked Witches anointing themselves preparatory to their departure for the Sabbat, but there are also illustrations of Witches *at* the Sabbat who are not naked but clothed. For interest I did a little research to see how many, if any, such early illustrations showed the Witches actually naked at the Sabbat. The result was fairly conclusive.

Hans Baldung Grun, the sixteenth Century German, did any number of Witch illustrations (*Witches at Work* and *Witches' Sabbat* are typical) all showing naked participants. Albrecht Dürer's *The Four Sorcerers* is of naked Witches. The Douce Collection, Bodleian Library, Oxford, contains an illustration of *The Witches' Sabbat On the Brocken* with many of the participants naked. Practically all of Goya's paintings of Witches show them naked (*Two Witches Flying On a Broom* being typical) and especially interesting is the 1613 (Paris) edition of Pierre de Lancre's *Tableau de l'inconstance des mauvais anges* which shows a great gathering of Witches with a circle of dancing nudes in one part and a nude mother presenting her equally naked child to the Horned God in another part.

It would seem, then, that there was no hard and fast rule. As is found today, some covens only strip when working magick but others wear loose robes. Other covens are naked throughout their rites.

The reasons for the nudity are several, but sex does not enter into it. Firstly, the nakedness is a sign of freedom, of a casting-off of worldly things. The ceremony of "Drawing Down the Moon," found in Gardnerian and some other tradi-

Witch riding on he-goat to the Walpurgisnacht

Albrecht Dürer

tions, contains some words said by the High Priestess, speaking as the Goddess:

> ...*and as a sign that ye be free ye shall be naked in your rites.*

But the most important reason for being skyclad is the belief in a power which comes from the human body. Some years ago Professor Otto Rahn, speaking at a meeting of the American Association for the Advancement of Science, described experiments he had conducted at Cornell University which showed conclusively that there are rays, emanations, powers, or what-you-will, that are emitted from certain parts of the human body (see also *Invisible Radiations of Organisms*, Rahn, Berlin, 1936). By experimenting he found that these rays were strong enough to kill yeast cells held, on a glass plate, close to the eye or to a pointing finger. Similar conclusions were reached and presented by Dr. Harold S. Burr, of Yale University, speaking at the Third International Cancer Congress.

Witches have always believed in a power emanating from the body and have developed ways to increase the production of this power, collect it, and use it to do what they term *magick*. That they do not know exactly what the power is does not matter for, as the British newspaper *The Western Morning News* (April 18, 1961) said in an article on faith-healing:

> The fact that natural forces can be used before people find scientifically what they are is not a case for dismissing them as imaginary. If it were, we should know nothing now about electricity and the structure of matter.

Theda Kenyon, in *Witches Still Live*, says:

> What is Witchcraft but the human control of natural forces through a supernatural power?…With fasting and incantation, with conjuring and sacrifice, men snare that power and use it—without actually knowing what it is that they use. So Witchcraft is the science of that power, within whose cult all mysteries merge and mingle.

In many covens Witches work in pairs, male and female, which might be compared to the positive and negative terminals of a battery. They are able to produce power which, by virtue of being produced *inside* the magick circle, is unable to escape. This power is then directed by the High Priestess to the desired purpose—frequently for works of healing. Although individuals can work magick, it is usually not as powerful as that which can be produced by a whole coven working together. There is here a "safety catch" against any Witch inclining to work negative magick—that which might hurt someone. The whole coven must be in accord, and must agree on the focus of the power, before any energy is raised and released. It has already been stated that, with the "threefold return" belief, a Witch would not be inclined to do any work of evil. Yet suppose a particular Witch *did* feel drawn to harm someone?—perhaps she has a short temper and has been "rubbed the wrong way" just once too often! She may be angry. She may feel the need to "get even." With the coven she must get the entire group—including the High Priestess—to feel as angry and as fired-up as she is in order to do any such negative work. This is a true safety catch. It is virtually impossible that she would so be able to influence all the others, especially the Elders of the coven. It is far more likely that her fellow coveners would calm her down and bring her back to her senses.

What sort of magick *is* done? Mainly works of healing, though not exclusively. Any one of them, looked at separately, could be dismissed with the word "coincidence." But coincidence is a handy word, much used whenever something appears unusual, incredible, or at all difficult to understand and explain. When large numbers of examples are produced, "coincidence" itself becomes a little strained. Witches have done sufficient to prove to themselves that what they do is not just coincidence. Whether or not anyone else believes them is unimportant—*they* believe. Here are a few examples (the names of the people concerned have been changed).

Frank's cousin Bill was in an auto accident. It was a bad smash and the outcome was, in the opinion of the medical experts, that Bill would never walk again. At twenty-two years of age the prospect of being bedridden, or at least confined to a wheelchair, was not a happy one for Bill, so Frank went to see some Witches. The Priestess promised nothing but, since the medical profession had given up, said they would certainly do what they could to help. Frank knew just how much Bill wanted to be his old self again, but he did not tell Bill what he had done since he knew there were no guarantees that the Witches could do anything. And, as another reason, he did feel a little silly for even believing in Witches!

Work was done by the coven over a period of time. There was no "wave of a wand, a bang and a flash"! It was six weeks later that Frank was working in his garage, at home, when he heard someone coming up the driveway behind him. Turning, he found it was

Bill. He was leaning heavily on a pair of sticks, but he was walking…grinning like a Cheshire cat as he moved toward his cousin.

Old Mr. Johnson, a widower, lived only for his garden. His flowers, his fruit trees, even his lawns were the pride of the neighborhood. But fruit trees attract small boys and small boys do not mind trampling on flowers to get to the fruit trees. Mr. Johnson's problem was that right next door to him lived a family with six boys in it. Six boys who were forever stealing his fruit and trampling his plants. Despite Mr. Johnson's protests, even threats, to the parents, the boys ran wild. Through a mutual acquaintance Mr. Johnson asked some Witches for help. Shortly afterward he had to go for a two-week visit to a relative. He shuddered to think of the state of his garden when he got back. But on his return he was surprised. From his other neighbors he learned that, quite suddenly, his tormentors had relocated. The father of the boys had been moved by his firm to another state. Next door to him Mr. Johnson found an empty house, shortly to be tenanted by a more respectable family.

Arthur had worked and studied hard for his finals. He had been up till the early hours of the morning each and every day for weeks. But despite his efforts he had had no time to really delve into one particular volume from which, every year, one or two important questions were always taken. In desperation Arthur consulted a friend of a friend, who happened to be a Witch. With the examination only three days away, the coven met and worked what magick they could. For the first time in twenty or more years, no questions appeared on the paper taken from the volume in question. Arthur passed, with honors.

These are but three brief examples of the type of magick done by Witches. The first two were worked by a New York coven, the other by a coven in Perth, Scotland. With regard to the last example, Witches believe that the gods help those who help themselves. If Arthur had just sat back and asked the Wica to get him through the exam, it is certain he would have failed. But he *had* worked, and hard. All that the Craft did was take care of the trimmings; he had handled the main part himself.

A point very much emphasized by members of the Craft, however, is that magick is always secondary. First and foremost the Wica is religion. Worship of the old gods will always come before anything else; magick is always secondary. If anyone wants to join a coven just so that they can work magick, they are trying to join for the wrong reason (and probably won't get in, at least not to a legitimate coven). If all you want to do is work magick then you don't *need* Witchcraft. Witchcraft is a religion, but magick is a practice; anyone can do—or attempt to do—magick. If that's your interest, then become a magician, not a Witch.

The circle in which the coven meets has a candle burning at each of the four cardinal points—north, east, south, and west. The altar, in the center, is usually oriented east-west so that the priest/ess standing before it is making his or her invocations to the north. (This is not true of all traditions, of course; some face east, or any of the directions.) On the altar are laid the *working tools* of the coven, which again will vary with traditions. Of these perhaps the most important is the sword, which is used to "cast the circle"; to consecrate the actual meeting place. In the old days when the coven was meeting outdoors, or even in a cottage

Wican altar, Saxon tradition

with a dirt floor, the sword would be stuck into the ground and, as the Priest walked around, he/she would literally mark the circle into which the coveners would move. In more modern times, with groups meeting in homes and apartments, the circle is usually marked with a piece of chalk or length of string ahead of time, to delineate the area to be used, but that line is still followed around with the sword to actually consecrate it.

A great deal of incense may be used at the meetings. Frequently Witches compound their own, though they do not hesitate to purchase the many excellent varieties generally available at religious supply stores. An old belief was that the smoke of the incense carried one's prayers up to the gods. This is still believed, but also the incense very definitely gives an ambience noticeably lacking without it.

Never do true Witches use drugs of any kind. The reason is simply that they are not necessary. Any self-styled "covens" who do use drugs are not truly Wican and are showing their lack of knowledge and abilities when it comes to the old ways. They should be avoided. From the incense, the peace and serenity, and the general atmosphere of the circle, a Witch obtains all the peace and contentment he or she could wish. There are no "trips" necessary; any psychic experiences can be obtained very easily without artificial stimulants, if the Witch has been properly trained.

This is not to say that Witches have *never* used drugs. They almost certainly did use them during the persecutions. But at that time they were meeting under extremely tense circumstances, with the chance of discovery and strong probability of a resultant loss of life. Drugs were almost certainly used at that time as a short cut to achieve that which can normally be acquired in the circle under ordinary circumstances. Today there is *no* excuse for a Witch to use drugs.

Whereas the tools on the altar are all *coven* tools, every Witch possesses an *athame* (pronounced "a-tham-ee"); the personal magickal tool. It is a knife, usually black-handled and with a double-edged blade. Many traditions have certain signs and symbols carved onto the handle. It is a magickal tool and not a weapon, so it should not be referred to as a dagger. Like all magickal tools, its fabrication follows certain guidelines and it is consecrated before use. In Witchcraft there are no blood sacrifices, so the athame is not used for any physical cutting.

Perhaps the most important possession of the coven is the Book of Shadows. This is a usually black-bound book (in the Saxon tradition it is bound in green) that contains all the rites and ceremonies of the tradition. There used to be only one copy of this for the coven, carefully kept by the Priestess. This again stems from the burning times, when it was important to keep all such items from falling into the wrong hands. Indeed the very name—Book of Shadows—comes from those times, when the Craft was having to meet "in the shadows." Prior to that the Craft was a purely oral tradition, with nothing written down. The rituals were only put into writing at that time so that, with the enforced separation of the covens, they would not be lost. When a Witch became a High Priestess she would copy, by hand, the book from her previous High Priestess, so that she would have one for her own coven. These days many individual Witches also keep their own book. It may not have everything in it that is in the coven book, but may just reflect the individual's personal interests and specialties, such as astrology, herbal lore, or healing. The book should always be handwritten, which imbues the book with power and *mana*. To have it typewritten or computer-generated may make it easier to read, but it is very unWitchlike and unmagickal and a definite "no-no"! Indeed, the title page of the book reads: "The Book of Shadows of the Witch Robat (for example) in his own hand of write" (i.e., his own handwriting).

The ceremonies of the Wica vary from tradition to tradition, but they all have the same basic formats, following the progress of the year. There are eight main festivals: four major Sabbats and four minor ones. These are frequently referred to as the Ceremonies of the Wheel, since they are equally-spaced around the year like the spokes of a wheel. In the same way Witches regard themselves as like the spokes of a wheel in the coven—all are equal and necessary, none being either first or last.

The four Greater Sabbats are: **Samhain** (pronounced "*Sow-en*"), November Eve, and the most important festival; the original new year. **Beltane**, May Eve, marking the other half of the year. Samhain and Beltane were the two which originally divided the year into halves, with the God of Hunting predominating during the winter months, or "dark half" of the year, and the Goddess predominating during the summer months, or "light half" of the year. **Imbolc**, February Eve, and **Lughnasadh**, August Eve, are the cross quarter days, dividing the year into four. In addition to these there are the four Lesser Sabbats which are the Spring and Autumn Equinoxes and the Summer and Winter Solstices.

In addition to these Sabbats there are the Esbats. These are the regular meetings of the coven. They occur at least at every full moon but—depending upon the individual coven—can be as often as once a week. It is at the Esbats that the work of the coven is done, the magick that might be needed. The Sabbats are strictly celebrations of the wheel of the year and no work should be done at these.

The rituals themselves vary from tradition to tradition as much as do the services of the multitude of Christian denominations (see the bibliography for books on a variety of traditions). But most follow the pattern of (1) consecrating the meeting place, (2) inviting the gods to attend, (3) prayers—asking for what is needed, (4) giving thanks for what has been received—which usually includes a ritual known as "Cakes and Wine," or "Cakes and Ale"; an acknowledgement of the gifts of the gods, and (5) a parting with the gods and closing of the Circle. If there is magick to be done it is done *after* the religious rites; after (4) and just before (5).

Witches do not proselytize. It is felt that if anyone really "belongs" to the Craft, then they will surely find it. Consequently it is not easy to "get into" Witchcraft if you have an interest. There are certainly far more covens scattered across this and other countries today than was the case ten or twenty years ago. Aidan Kelly (*Crafting the Art of Magic, Book I*, Llewellyn, 1991) puts the number at 5,000 covens in the United States, 200,000 Witches and Pagans in North America. Yet still, covens are not easy to locate—due to the continuing persecution of the Old Religion by those still ignorant of its true form. Most people will try to track down a local group by making inquiries at their nearest bookstore, be it "New Age," "Metaphysical," or everyday run-of-the-mill. Booksellers usually have a very good finger on the pulse of their area and know their regular customers and their special interests. They can usually point an inquiring mind in the right direction.

One group which has spent years developing a network and has earned a wonderful reputation in their local area, not to mention nationally, is Circle Sanctuary (P.O. Box 219, Mount Horeb, WI 53572). Led by Selena Fox and Dennis Carpenter, they publish a periodical (*Circle Network News*), which is one of the longest-lived of Pagan journals, together with annual guides to Pagan groups and arts, directories, bulletins; they sponsor festivals and retreats and train Pagan priesthood.

Some searchers will advertise in a New Age journal—the above mentioned *Circle Network News*, Llewellyn's *New Worlds of Mind and Spirit*, and *Fate* magazine are just a few. This can work but should be done cautiously. For example, do not give out your home address but use a post office box. Use only your first name, or your proposed Craft name. Arrange to initially meet anyone on neutral, public ground, such as at a restaurant, until you really get to know them and feel you can trust them. Because of the many hundreds of years of Christian propaganda, presenting such horrendous misconceptions of what Witchcraft is, a large number of unsavory characters get attracted to it. If you are sincere in your desire to join the Old Religion, you definitely do not want to cross the paths of these "weirdos"! Hence the caution. You need to ascertain that others who profess the same interests really do have them. Ask them lots of questions and get them to ask lots of questions of you. You can tell a great deal by what someone asks. Find out what books they have read on the subject (see the bibliography at the back of this book for recommended works on Witchcraft) and what they think of those books.

There are people operating what they term "Witchcraft covens" which are no such thing, or which are the Satanic variety which has no connection with true Witchcraft. Do not get trapped into one of these. *Witchcraft is a positive, nature-based religion of brotherly and sisterly love.* If you find you are being told to do things which are not in your best interests, if you are being ordered around by a frustrated dictator, if you are encouraged to do *anything* which would harm yourself or another...run, don't walk, away from there.

10: ROOTS OF MODERN WICA

But is Wica really a descendant of the Old Religion in an unbroken line, as Gerald Gardner and others have claimed? Did covens really continue to exist, in secret, all the time from the days of the persecutions through to the twentieth century?

Gardner claimed that the coven into which he was initiated, in the late 1930s, was such a coven. It was led by "Old Dorothy" Clutterbuck-Fordham and was located in the New Forest, Hampshire. Doreen Valiente has admitted to authoring much of the Gardnerian Book of Shadows which Gardner presented in the 1950s. But what of that original coven?

In his book, *Crafting the Art of Magic*, Aidan Kelly makes a large number of assumptions to try to back up his theory that the whole Wican idea was put together—invented—by a group of people, including Gardner, one night in 1939:

> In September 1939, probably on the 28th, the evening of the full moon, Gerald Gardner, Dorothy Clutterbuck Fordham, Dafo, and others of their occult circle of friends were, I believe, sitting in Dorothy's living room, discussing England's perilous state, now at war with Germany. Was England in danger of perishing spiritually for want of a truly native British religion they could all believe in? Gardner, at least, had been thinking for years about how to go about creating one. Encouraged by the tension of that moment, they decided to create the "witch cult of western Europe" described by Margaret Murray.

To quote Kelly's own words against him, on this particular point, "an argument from probabilities cannot be convincing."

Whether or not modern Wica was totally invented by Gardner and others will probably never be known for sure, however it must be admitted as a strong possibility. But there is still another possibility that, yes, there *was* an existing coven into which Gardner was initiated...though if so, there is virtually nothing left of its writings.

Whatever the truth of those earlier days it is certain that over a period of years Gardner adopted and adapted a large variety of material from many different sources, put together with Doreen Valiente's excellent original compositions, to make up his own Book of Shadows. This is what is presented today as Gardnerian Wica.

Nothing else has emerged, in the contemporary Witchcraft scene, that has been able to show a provable line of descent from earlier times. Charles Godfrey Leland's *Aradia: Gospel of the*

Gerald Gardner and his High Priestess,
Monique Wilson (Lady Olwen)

Witches of Italy was quite different in content from the Gardnerian *Book of Shadows* (although the latter included sections "borrowed" from the former).

Shortly after Gardner presented Wica to the world others came running out, making similar claims to ancient Wican heritage. Alex Sanders (who was actually initiated in 1963) claimed to have been initiated as a child, by his grandmother—the "grandmother initiation" claim was immediately picked up on by others and is still used today by numerous would-be Witches—but he could only present variations on the Gardnerian Book of Shadows. Leo Martello's "Sicilian Wicca" was a combination of Leland and Gardner. Others have been completely unable to provide anything approaching proof that theirs is truly the unbroken continuation of the ancient religion.

It would seem, then, that there is no *unbroken* tradition. That Wica was a religion of old is certain, as we have seen in the previous pages and has been detailed by Murray and others. But that there have been covens in the second half of the twentieth century who have an unbroken lineage seems unlikely.

Not that this matters, of course. *If Gardner had made up the whole thing, basic idea and all, from scratch, it would not negate Wica as a viable religion today. Its rapid growth around the world attests to its "rightness" in terms of people's religious needs.*

With the publication of Gardner's books there was, indeed, an almost immediate recognition by many that here was what they had been looking for…even if most had not realized they had been looking. A balance between a male deity and a female deity, a belief in reincarnation, retribution in this life, a closeness and harmony with nature, a do-only-good philosophy—these were all tenets which were presented to the world at just the right time, and the world responded.

The only problem was that so many people suddenly wanted to become Witches, but covens were still few and far between. Even if one could make contact with a coven there was that long waiting period before initiation. It was a necessary waiting period, of course, because of the many misconceptions which still abounded that drew the unsavory element as well as the sincere seekers. This was very much the case in the United States,

Wican Priest's horned helmet

and part of the reason—in this author's opinion—for the decline and fall of Gardnerian Wica.

Gardner received letters from many people all around the world, all wanting to make contact with a coven. With the final establishment of a coven in New York (an offshoot of Gardner's own coven, led by Lady Olwen in Perth, Scotland), by myself, in the beginning of 1964, all such letters from this side of the Atlantic were forwarded to that coven. This author was High Priest of the coven; Lady Rowen was High Priestess. Founding members were Maverick, Jonet, Reinhart, Lilith, Skyld, Morven, Sea, and Deidra, to use their Wican names.

Over a period of years others were brought into the coven and other covens sprang from this mother one: Morag and Ketryn started the first Canadian coven; Theos and Thain took Gardnerian Wica down to Louiseville, Kentucky; Sea and

Deidra took it to New Jersey; Froniga and Wayland to California, and so on.

But the problem was that the teachings that had been given were strictly followed and, consequently, it took a long time to initiate new people. And when people get a taste of something they want—they don't want to wait! By the mid-1960s more books had been published, including Doreen Valiente's *Where Witchcraft Lives*, T. C. Lethbridge's *Witches*, Kittredge's *Witchcraft in Old and New England*, Eric Maple's *Dark World of Witches*, Robbins's *The Encyclopedia of Witchcraft and Demonology* and—significantly—Ira Levin's *Rosemary's Baby*. Perhaps more significant than the book was the movie of *Rosemary's Baby*. Through ignorance (we must presume), Levin referred to the characters in his book as Witches. In actual fact they were Satanists, and it wouldn't have made any difference to the book to have called them by the correct name. But, unfortunately for the embryonic Wican movement, he called them Witches and consequently hundreds if not thousands of people decided that they would start "covens" and become "Witches"...just like in the book/movie!

Groups of self-styled Witches started springing up all over the place. True and sincere seekers after the Wica that Gardner and Murray had extolled were sidetracked, many being taken into pseudo-covens and given an irreversible dose of negative Witchcraft that would drive them from the true Craft forever.

Where there were true Gardnerian covens, there was also tremendous pressure put upon the leaders to bring in those who were hammering at their doors. Many weakened. The year-and-a-day between degrees that had worked so well and had contributed to keeping a negative element out of the Craft, went by the board.

This author was severely criticized for being "snooty," since it seemed the original New York coven was being "overly selective"!

With the bringing-in, and raising through the degrees, of those who probably should not have been advanced (let alone those who should never even have been brought in!), it was not long before the ego trip became a major factor in the Craft. "I'm a more important Witch than you!" "I have more covens than you have!" and similar petty powerplays became obvious. Degrees were handed out as though they were so much candy. It was said of one Priestess that if anyone happened to slow down when driving past her house, she would run out and initiate them!

As Kelly points out, a religion will grow and develop. It will incorporate changes, and this is usually all to the good. But such changes usually come about slowly, evolving rather than appearing as a contagion. Regrettably the Craft scene in America, in the early 1970s, was such that (for example) one New York area Priestess, in an attempt to be *the* Witch Queen and have multiple covens, was advancing people at a tremendous rate and then giving out different adulterated versions of her Book of Shadows to each of her new Priestesses. The contents were slanted to make the new Priestesses completely reliant upon her, even forbidding them to initiate anyone without her blessing! (It seems she never stopped to think that, at some future date, some of these Priestesses might get together and compare their books!) Similarly horrendous things were happening in other places so that, today, there are many descendants of these covens who feel they have fine lineage but are, in fact, no more "Gardnerian" than their neighboring eclectic groups. The degree system, which should have worked well, collapsed. (This was part of the reason that this author left Gardnerian Wica at that time.)

But, as with most things, time brought about a settling of the troubled waters. Whether "officially" or "unofficially," a large number of people were now Wicans. And along with the undesirables were many, many desirables—many who were sincere in their desires and designs, many who had studied and learned and who had much to offer. A wide variety of "traditions" (something of a misnomer for newly created denominations!) appeared, offering something for everyone. In all religion a variety of styles of worship is called for if everyone is to feel comfortable. Some people like a great deal of pomp and ritual; others prefer simpler fare; still others prefer just the rudiments of worship. So it is within Wica. Similarly, some people have a particular background, be it ethnic or whatever, and prefer their religious worship to fit to that background. Today there are Keltic groups, Saxon groups, Druidic, Scottish, Egyptian, Dianic, Fairy, Norse, Feminist, and a host of others, including innumerable "eclectic" groups.

In the next chapter we will look at Wica today and where it seems to be going in the future.

11: WHITHER WICA?

Wica is one of the fastest growing religions today. According to Aidan Kelly, the numbers of Wicans and other Neopagans in the United States exceed those of Quakers, Unitarians, and Buddhists.

Many groups are now "churches," on a par with any church of any other denomination or persuasion. Tremendous strides have been made with the establishing of "legal" covens, in the sense of those that are recognized by the Internal Revenue Service as nonprofit religious organizations. And Wica is recognized at a federal level by its inclusion in the Department of the Army Pamphlet No. 165–13: *Religious Requirements and Practices of Certain Selected Groups—a Handbook for Chaplains*. This includes instructions as to the religious rights of Wicans in the Armed Forces. They are listed alongside Islamic groups, Sikhs, Christian Heritage, Indian Heritage, Japanese, and Jewish groups.

In Britain the Pagan Federation is very active and has been largely instrumental in Wica becoming officially recognized as a religion by British prison authorities, with Wican ministers being appointed to prisons.

For some years now there have been public and semiprivate festival celebrations across the United States, some of them numbering as many as a thousand participants. Wicans hold conventions in modern hotels and convention buildings, many of these becoming popular annual affairs. Wican clergy are to be found on ecumenical councils, visiting Wicans in hospitals and penitentiaries, lecturing at colleges and universities.

Yet there is still persecution, with individual Witches being fired from their jobs, chased out of town, harassed and degraded. As mentioned earlier, the fundamentalist Christians tend to have a mind-lock on the Middle Ages when it comes to acknowledging the religious rights of others.

With a view to obtaining a broader perspective on Wicans' views of what the future may hold, one or two prominent Wicans/Pagans were approached and asked to contribute to this book. It is with gratitude, and honor, that this author presents the thoughts of Ed Fitch, Michael Ragan, and Selena Fox.

Wicca — Yesterday, Today and Tomorrow
Ed Fitch

Wicca, according to a few commentators who seem to know, is said to be statistically the fastest-growing religion in the United States and perhaps in the world. All this has happened largely unnoticed or ignored—as well as generally misunderstood—by the media and by government. Which is probably just as well, since historical precedent seems to indicate that official sanctioning by an established power group can have a disastrous effect on a young movement, by quashing it, driving it underground, or by twisting it to serve its own goals.

Wicca is, by its very nature, a creed which honors the Earth. Rather than having a harsh Old Testament directive to dominate and be the terror of all other creatures and to view the world as evil, Wiccans instead view the earth as the very personification of humankind's original and still pre-eminent deity. As such, Wicca is precisely in line with today's most perceptive thinkers in caring for our planet and its variegated ecology.

Another most fundamental tenet of the Craft is that the Godhead is by its very nature both female and male. In addition to very beautiful, sensual, and magical Goddess- and God-imagery, this pre-eminent theological point requires an equal balance between male and female in the priesthood, in the coven membership, and even in the relations between the various members of Wiccan and Pagan groups. As such, Wicca and Neo-paganism are in the forefront of a very major and permanent change in today's advanced societies. There is even a tendency to be matrifocal in reaction to our civilization's overly long and harsh patriarchal tradition...which itself can be traced back to Wicca's oldest and major adversary, Christianity.

A bit of clarification of terms is in order here. All Wiccans are Neo-pagans, but Neo-pagans are not necessarily Wiccans *(as all Catholics are Christians but not all Christians are Catholics—RB)*. As the movement has grown in this country and abroad, the numbers of Wiccans—those interested in delving into the mysteries that surround life, death, and the turnings of the natural world—has grown vastly. Much greater in number, however, are those who are not necessarily inclined toward studying magic in theory and practice but who nonetheless subscribe to a worldview which honors the Earth and seeks to be at peace with Nature and acknowledges the Ancient Gods. As such the Neopagans and the Witches are close allies.

Gardnerian Wicca spearheaded the coming of the Old Religion to North America during the 1960s. There have been quite a lot of spin-offs and adaptions under other names and, in the far western part of the United States, there is a lively growth of local varieties which claim the name of "Gardnerian" but which in fact have been researched and developed locally. While not really the true Gardnerian corpus of rituals and traditions, most tend to be quite good in ceremonial quality and should really be considered to be parallel varieties of Wicca in their own right.

The coming of the Gardnerian Craft also had the side effect of encouraging other local family, or semi-ethnic, traditions to "come out of the closet" and gave them a standard to compare against and to fill out any areas where their surviving lore was lacking. Some traditions were assembled whole cloth by founders with varying degrees of talent and scholarship, many of them claiming extreme (if unverifiable) antiquity. The means of testing the validity of these traditions has come to be realized by many as something quite simple: if a tradition's magic works, it's valid; if not, it's invalid. It has proven to be that simple!

Wicca appeared in the mid-1960s as an ancient Western-oriented alternative to Christianity. As such it was embraced by parts of the counterculture movement of the late '60s and underwent an explosive growth, in the process becoming linked more firmly with a young, well-educated demographic group. While the radical politics of that era have (fortunately) faded to a middle-of-the-road, middle-American ethos, the impressive gains of the Craft have not just remained but have continued expanding.

Interestingly enough, some of the first and most influential Wiccans instrumental in spreading the Craft were in the Army, Navy, and Air Force. A person who is in the military has always been likely to be one who seeks adventure, travel, new sights, and new ideas. Gardnerian Wicca, and others, have been helped to spread in Europe in general, and Germany in particular, by members of the U.S. military. In their tours of duty the servicemen and women have begun by practicing the Old Ways in their military housing quarters, then usually off-base on the local economy where more privacy would be available. The American Witches, of course, were interested in the natural beauty and the traditions of their host country. In time they met locals with similar, if unstated, interests. Friendships led to initiations and a natural growth of the initially small covens. In this way rituals were exchanged and what had started and developed in England and America linked up with what was found in continental Europe.

With the fall of the Communist Bloc there has been a considerable flow of Wicca and Neo-paganism into Eastern Europe and Russia, though little is known about it as yet. *(There have been at least two Saxon covens established in Moscow over the past ten years.—RB)* A few tantalizing words have crept through the media on this matter, by reporters who have no idea of what is really going on.

There has been a trend on the part of some Wiccans to bring in the Norse pantheon to their religion. Asatru, or Odinism, has a particularly strong ethos of protection of one's family, kindred, and extended family against the threats of a hostile outer world.

Given the painfully obvious decline, and even decay, in today's society, Pagans as much as, or more than, other citizens are coming to realize that friends, extended families, and children must be protected from the rising tide of arrogant savagery on the streets.

Celtic has long been a favorite of Wiccans, and indeed much work has been done in recovering the ancient magical traditions and reconstituting the archaic rites of England, Ireland, Scotland, and Wales. Large groups, such as the Roebucks in Southern California and a great variety of Celtic groups in the San Francisco Bay area, have grown and spread greatly over the last twenty years, and promise even greater growth in the future.

Wicca and Paganism have resulted in a continually-growing corpus of researched and reconstructed lore, rituals, traditions, historical studies, and more. The richness of all this material further enriches the Craft, and the spiritual spiral thus continues upward to higher and yet higher levels as the scholarship of many Wiccans and their friends continues.

Wicca in its many branches and traditions, as well as the "non-denominational" Neo-paganism which has grown up in association with it, represents nothing more nor less than the continuing attempt at culmination of our deeply-ingrained seeking for our European roots. We have long known, sometimes intuitively (and sometimes in sharp brilliance in the writings of Tolkien, Howard, and others), that our own ancient past held magic and power that would fulfill the soul and swell our pride. Wicca has given us back this solid foundation, and it has returned us to our old gods—the ones who grew with our archaic ancestors over a thousand, thousand generations.

Yet Wicca is for today. There is a growing realization in high tech areas, such as computer hardware and software, that many of the "wild cards" — the brilliant young "movers and shakers" in the industry—are "techno-Pagans" who have their feet in a tradition older than the human race but with their heads and hands in the present and the future. The U.S. space program was perhaps one of the first professional areas where Witches and Pagans started to find their niches. They have spread from there.

Techno-Pagans, who know their computers as well as they know their magic, laughingly refer to themselves as "wizards"... which indeed they are, for corporations depend upon their unsurpassed expertise and co-workers come to them to solve problems that are beyond all others. Their wit and high intelligence has gained them the comradeship of atheists and agnostics—who are also found abundantly in high-technology industries, it seems—who view them as almost kindred souls. The attitude is, "You're smart and unconventional and good company. If the Fundamentalists come after you tomorrow, they'll be after me the next day!" In sheer playfulness and for profit the computer games they design have caught the imagination of an entire generation of kids, teenagers, and adults.

And where is the Craft of the Wise going in the future? It is likely that Wicca will, before too many years, become widespread enough that its adherents will be in enough positions to affect not just the arts and sciences but the courses of governments and multinational corporations as well. The result would be a calming effect of increased tolerance and understanding over human affairs, and an ever-increasing effect of honoring the Earth as more and more effective public policy. The existing religious structures, which until now have only made occasional grumbles about the return of an antagonist which outclasses them in every way, will have to be persuaded or compelled to accept that freedom of religion is here to stay. But by that time enough Wiccans and Pagans should have gravitated to suitably high positions in industry and politics to assure that this does indeed happen. With a (thoroughly Pagan) balanced and honest liking of one's fellow human ("I'll extend fellowship to you, but you must deserve it!") and a deep love of nature, added to an enjoyment of the challenges that science can bring, the world can only become better. Even if a time of troubles must come first—as it may—Wicca will cause events to ultimately improve.

Tomorrow, the world. The next day...to the stars themselves! But that, friends, will be another story.

Witchcraft from My Viewpoint
Michael Ragan

Where is Wicca today and where is it going? I'm not sure any of us really knows! But from where I sit I do see some hopeful changes. Sadly, I also see many of the old negatives.

One major factor which could be construed as either positive or negative, depending upon one's personal view, is that of the "changing of the guard." For better or worse the old leaders fade and are replaced by the new. To me, the new guard seems a bit more outspoken and, for the most part, a bit more politically astute. They seem more willing to stand up and be counted but at the same time are more likely to try to work within the system than confront it head-on. Unfortunately I also see a few egos in the new ranks that seem determined to continue the conflicts of old.

Another area that has seemingly gotten out of hand is the organization. My purpose in establishing the Temple (of

Danaan) was merely to provide a teaching platform. However, more and more people are stepping forward asking to be a part of "the Clan"! Consequently we have made provisions for accepting members either singly or in groups.

On the positive side I am heartened by a growing interest in "spiritual roots." This seems to be especially so with those of Celtic heritage. At the same time the body of works dealing with Celtic lore is expanding to meet that interest. Regretfully, some of the new works reflect poor or incomplete research by the author.

Also favorable is what seems to be a trend for many to "come out of the closet" and be counted. There was an incident in Jonesboro, Arkansas, in the summer of 1993, when a couple opened a "Witchcraft store" and were consequently evicted by their landlord. The resulting march of Witches through the city streets on Lammas contained many who had never before dared to publicly proclaim their faith. One can only admire those who go against every instinct to publicly march as a Witch in the middle of the "Bible Belt." I doubt that such a display would have occurred ten years ago, or even five years ago.

I also seem to detect a growing desire by many to band together with those of like mind. In the Temple of Danaan* we have had to make provisions for admission to permanent membership not only to those who have studied with us, but also to those who have come to know us within the community and wish to remain associated even though they are not "Irish" or even "Celtic." I think the response among the Arkansas Craft at Jonesboro was partially motivated by this growing feeling of kinship.

---

*Michael Ragan is the founder and leader of the Temple of Danaan, one of the leading Irish traditions of Wica (P. O. Box 765, Hanover, IN 47243).

Whither Witchcraft?
Selena Fox

It is important for Witches and other Pagans to have interfaith dialogue, not only with Christians but also with people of all other faiths. Such dialogue should focus not on who has the better theology but on how we can work together to address the many problems on this planet. Through dialogue we can understand the diversity within our religious movements and build alliances to uphold religious freedom, to improve the environment, and to bring spiritual healing to Planet Earth.

I was recently a speaker at a theological conference* on religious freedom held at Chicago Theological Seminary. Most of the people attending that conference were Protestant ministers, Catholic priests, theologians from universities from all parts of the country, and religious scholars. At this conference we examined persecutions of minority religions and brainstormed ways that people can work together to correct this problem. It isn't just Witches who are having problems in this day and age.

I am optimistic about the future for the Craft and other forms of Paganism, especially if humankind becomes more environmentally responsible and more willing to work in harmony within its own diversity and with other life forms. One of the growths in the Craft and Paganism over the past thirty years is in its diversity. The Craft has influenced the following types of nature religion: Animism, Earth-centered Spirituality, Ecofeminism, Goddess

---

*Selena Fox, as a co-founder of Circle Sanctuary, is one of the leading figures in Wica today in fighting for religious freedom. She attends many national and international interfaith conferences working tirelessly for religious freedom, environmental responsibility, and spiritual healing.

Spirituality, Green Spirituality, Nature Spirituality, Paganism and Neo-paganism, Pantheism, Polytheism, and Shamanism.

In the next century I can see Witchcraft developing and expanding. I have long been working to manifest what I envision, as have others, but much will depend upon how well Wiccans are able to work together to achieve the goals we share.

Some of what I would like to see come about is as follows: I would like Nature religions to free themselves from the dungeon of religious oppression and be respected as safe, honorable, and legal forms of spiritual expression, fully acknowledged and respected by religious scholars, anthropologists, physicians, psychotherapists, and others. Wiccan ministers should receive equal respect, equal access, and equal treatment as ministers of other religions receive in ministering to those in hospitals, prisons, asylums, homeless shelters, rape crisis centers, hospices, and other institutions. And Witches should be able to do their rituals and practice their religion without harassment or any form of interference from others.

There should be an end to religious discrimination against Wiccans, for jobs, housing, and the like. There should be well-funded Wiccan legal centers in existence until such discrimination is abolished.

I would like to see dictionaries, encyclopedias, and other works accurately describe contemporary Witchcraft and remove inaccurate and misleading statements. They should also capitalize the words referring to Nature religions, just as they do for other religions (e.g., Witchcraft, Wicca, Paganism, Druidism, and so on). I would like to see Goddess temples, Wiccan churches, and other Pagan religious organizations listed alongside Unitarian Universalist societies, Christian churches, and

Jewish synagogues in telephone books, newspaper listings, dictionary and encyclopedia entries, and similar reference works.

More interfaith dialogue, association, and commitment to work together, by Witches, Pagans, and practitioners of other religions and spiritual paths, should work toward all forms of media presenting the positive nature of Wicca, in respectful, accurate, and educational ways. Hopefully more Witch and Pagan celebrities would then be able to come out into the open.

Circle Sanctuary's ministry continues (P. O. Box 219, Mt. Horeb, WI 53572), with demand for our services ever increasing—perhaps a sign that some of what I hope for, above, will finally come about. In the next century we plan to expand our academic research and publishing as well as our counseling and psychotherapy services. Our religious freedom work will continue, but I hope the need to go into courts to uphold religious freedom for the Craft will diminish as our religious movement becomes better understood and accepted. I view the inclusion of five Wiccan and/or Pagan organizations in the circle of sponsors of the 1993 Parliament of the World's Religions as a sign that more acceptance is happening in the halls of religion in the U.S.A. and elsewhere. We will continue to do interfaith work and interfaith dialogue, and facilitation of multicultural interfaith rituals will continue as part of my ministry as a Wiccan Priestess.

12: THE TEEN INTEREST PLUS FEMINIST WICA

As an author I get a lot of mail from readers. Many letters are from teenagers who have found what they are looking for, religiously, in Witchcraft, but are having a hard time convincing parents and friends that it is a benign religion that will not lead them into drugs and trafficking with the Devil. No coven today will accept and initiate an underage person who is not the child of one of its present coven members. With the rash of charges of physical and sexual abuse promulgated by well-meaning or over-enthusiastic self-appointed guardians of the young, it is no wonder that anyone in any way connected with underage children is hesi-tant to make any sort of a move not previously overseen and approved by the children's parents. Although understandable to an extent, where religion is concerned this is unfortunate. Where the Old Religion is concerned, it is doubly unfortunate due to the need to first overcome misconceptions.

Teenagers are the future of the Craft. They should be allowed access to the religion of their choice. Llewellyn Publications (P. O. Box 64383, St. Paul, MN 55164-0383) produces a bimonthly publication called *Llewellyn's New Worlds of Mind and Spirit*. In the Sep/Oct 1993 edition of the magazine, editor Jana Branch put together a number of letters that she had received from teenaged readers, addressing this problem. With her permission I here reproduce what they had to say.

Rachel from Connecticut wrote: "My parents are Jehovah's Witnesses, and I'm 16. They are unaware of my studies in Wicca, Paganism and magick. These are hard and difficult times for me. I hope to hear from any readers who have or do live with parents who are intolerant of their Pagan practices."

New Worlds was *overwhelmed* by the number of reader responses to Rachel's quandary, not only from adults with advice but from other teens in the same situation. The theme in most letters was *perseverance* and *patience*, and a hearty "You are not alone!"

Michelle, from Houston, Texas, wrote: "When I read your letter my heart went out to you. I was in your shoes over ten years ago when I was 13 years old and beginning my journey to the world of Wicca. Please know that if you truly feel that Wicca and Paganism is in your heart and soul, then do not abandon your studies of the Craft. There is no law that says you have to follow your parents' beliefs, but if you can show them that you respect their religion, in time they may be able to do the same. It's also okay to stand up for what you believe in, and in no way does that mean that you don't love your parents."

Emily in Sacramento writes: "I am also 16, a magician in training in the midst of a Christian residential suburban nightmare. I suggest you find other people you can talk to, so that the secret will really only be held from your parents. Holding things in is rarely constructive. It also serves to make you feel more isolated; alone."

David, in North Carolina, writes: "I am 16, and my parents don't want me practicing magick. I have fooled them into thinking that the books I read and study are for my career as a parapsychologist. The key is patience. In a couple of years you will be an adult. These next few years will be agonizing. You will prevail though."

Morgaine, from Ohio, wrote some practical advice: "When I began practicing Wicca I, too, was living under my parents' roof. I remember feeling alone, frustrated, incomplete. I want you to know that you are *not* alone, and that someday it will all be worth the difficulty you must deal with now. For now, though, here are some hints to help you along:—

"Do your parents require you to attend with them when they worship? If so, use the time to educate yourself by listening for parallels and similarities between your beliefs and theirs. You can meditate on this while you pray. At home, write these down in your Book of Shadows. When it comes time, someday, for you to help your parents understand your ways, you will have a list they will be able to relate to. It will be easier for them to understand that 'there are many paths to the center', and that your path and theirs are not so very far apart after all.

"Are you having trouble enjoying a Sabbat when an altar is too dangerous to set up in your room? I had this problem. Now there is nothing like a great Sabbat celebration, but you don't have to watch it blow past either. I found that I could visualize and meditate my way through an entire ritual, and thoroughly enjoy a Sabbat sitting skyclad on my bed! It is not easy at first, trying to keep a picture of my altar, the decorations, all the details at the same time; just ground and center well and keep the energy flowing. This is excellent exercise; you will need this ability later anyway.

"Don't ever feel bad for being secretive; not so long ago your life would have depended on it! Use these difficult times to remember that it was even harder during the Burning Times, and that our sisters before us made even greater sacrifices so that we may practice today."

Chris, in Ohio, writes: "My heart goes out to you. I have been a secretly practicing Wiccan for 10 years, for the sake of my husband's medical practice. One of my greatest gifts from Wicca is finding joy and magic (divinity) in the things of everyday life.

"I have an altar in my bedroom that, to the untrained eye, simply looks like an interesting collection of knick-knacks. No one suspects that the large stuffed plush cougar on my bed is a symbol of my power animal or that my three cats are really my familiars. I like to cook, and who would know that the wooden spoon and silver knife on my wall are really my wand and athame?

"I stay tuned to the seasons. My Jack-o'-lantern looks like everyone else's, as does the autumn wreath I hang on my door on September 21 or so. Only my deities and I quietly smile at the significance.

"We each must find our own path, and what I have shared may not be for you. Three truths for me: (i) Magic does not come from external symbols. *True* magic comes from a pure heart. (ii) Divinity can be found in the objects of *everyday* life, and (iii) our spiritual *intent* is most important. Do we reach out to help others, our community and our Earth (be it animal humane efforts, conservation or stopping the prejudice surrounding victims of AIDS)? *Living* Wicca is the true magic, for in doing so we transform ourselves and the world."

Morrigan-Aa, in New Jersey, writes: "My basic advice is don't give up! Your dilemma brings me back to when I first became a Witch at the age of 12 (now I'm 18). One thing I remember is that I could never have what some term the 'appropriate' tools. My first chalice was a paper cup, my athame was a steak-knife, 'cakes and ale' was fruit juice and cheese puffs!

"In actuality you need none of those things, not even physical substitutes. Use visualization and the gifts of Mother Earth. For example, a candle symbolizes fire, the light of sun, moon and star. If you have no candles, feel the solar heat, the blood racing within, the icy stars above. They are the same. Tools are merely symbols and books merely a guide to the path's beginning. Always remember that Wicca is not a set of rituals bound by restrictions but life itself, a spiritual rejoicing that never falters during the course of your life, no matter how terrible the persecution."

Maerwyn, in New Hampshire, wrote: "I can give you only one piece of good advice. Do what your heart tells you to do."

Larrise, in Indiana, wrote: "Arm yourself with information and truth. Be honest. Think of what your parents might say against your studies and formulate answers to educate them while defending yourself and Wicca. Put yourself on the offensive—nicely—with the least amount of negative confrontation you can manage. Call on Her for aid."

Sixteen-year-old Andrea wrote: "I really don't have any advice for Rachel, but it was a relief to know that some young people like me feel and think the same."

Thirteen-year-old Acacia writes: "My father is Catholic and my mom is Lutheran. I stumbled upon Wicca about a year ago. In January, on my birthday, as a gift to myself I dedicated to Solitary Wicca. I was very happy, except for the fact that I had to keep quiet about it. In February I joined a computer BBS and met many other Pagans who gave me advice. I have found great comfort in talking to them.

"Now I have found three occult, Pagan, Wiccan, New Age stores where I found like-minded people to talk to once in a while."

So it can be seen that, no matter your age or situation, with patience you can get around the obstacles and still be a part of Wica, the Old Religion.

In *Buckland's Complete Book of Witchcraft*, I outline a way of tackling the problem of being asked, by parents, spouse, boyfriend, or girlfriend, "Are you a Witch?" The basic rule here is to throw the question back onto the other party: "What do you mean by 'Witch'?" This way you can find out what preconceptions he or she has and then set out to correct them. As much as possible get your "opponent"—if that's not too strong a word—to read as much as possible. It's amazing how impressive the printed word can be to many people. In the bibliography that is at the end of this present volume, I give a listing of those books I particularly recommend, along with a variety of others on the subject. Direct your questioner to these books. Tell them "If you're *really* interested to know what I believe in, then please take the time to read this." If they expect you to honor their beliefs, they should be willing to honor yours.

Of the Wica we have discussed so far in this book, there is a branch that has been making considerable headway and is obviously filling a long-felt need in today's society. That branch is Feminist Wica.

Many Wicans believe, as does this author, that as a religion of nature there needs to be a balance between male and female. Gardnerians, and others, think this has to be a strict equality (numbers of males and females in a coven, for example), whereas many others, including this author, do not see nature generally as being quite that precise. However, the fact remains that most traditions do acknowledge a Goddess *and* a God. There is a feeling that we need to get away from the harsh patriarchy of Christianity but, at the same time, the pendulum should not swing completely in the other direction, for that would be equally inequitable.

Feminists, however, disagree. For them there is acknowledgement of the Goddess to the total exclusion of the God. Their covens are made up entirely of women and they are very happy in that state. And this, perhaps, should be the bottom line. As has been said previously, religion is a very personal thing. To be entirely satisfying to the individual it must fulfill all that individual's requirements. If it does that, then it does not behoove anyone else to criticize. On that note, then, I am delighted to have my dear friend Zsuzsanna "Z" Budapest tell a little of Women's Mysteries.

Inside Women's Mysteries
Zsuzsanna Budapest*

"When the Moon Goddess Diana fell in love with the Sun Goddess Lucina their daughter was Aradia, the first female avatar in our times. Upon the request of the moon, Aradia manifested herself as a human woman and came amongst the people teaching Witchcraft. It was at a time when there were too many poor people in jails unjustly; when the landlords abused their powers and oppressed the working poor. Our avatar Aradia came and gathered the women and taught them the mysteries, the esbats and blessings and cursings, using the power of the moon."

This legend is at the core of our Dianic Tradition today. Once again times are very bad. Women are attacked every second by men, in our patriarchal society. Children get raped and abused, wars rage senselessly. It's time to lift our collective female will against the abusers, hence the rebirth of the Dianic Tradition in the 'seventies; lifted upon the mighty back of the phenomenon called "women's liberation." We claimed back the moon and the sun! "Take back the night and take back the jobs!" Take back the future. Women's Mysteries encountered fierce opposition even within the Craft.

The Women's Mysteries traditions were alive and limping even through into the fourth century. We knew about the rites of Athena, initiations of seven-year-old girls, bear dancers, schools of Artemis—even some Aphrodisian temples were in

---

* Z. Budapest is one of the original moving forces behind the Feminist Wican movement. She has authored a number of popular books on various aspects of Women's Mysteries (see Bibliography).

operation, as we know from Euripides' plays. The Vestal Virgins, keepers of the flame, survived into Roman times, though not much past it.

The dramatic destruction of the shrine of the two Goddesses at Eleusys, by the new Christians, signaled the end of the Goddess culture in Europe...until this century.

When I joined the Women's Movement, religion/spirituality was a blindspot of the collective female psyche. Women couldn't decide if it was political to be spiritual. Too much oppression had been perpetrated through this media, religion. Women were suspicious and rightly so. Wasn't it "God's word" that made them inferior? A vessel? The Devil's playmate? The weaker sex? Sinners burdened with guilt of the original sin? How could anything erase that kind of shame?

My work was a conscious reclaiming of the Goddess and her female mysteries. I had to infuse this inherited Witchcraft tradition with modern feminism if I wanted to be part of the new culture of women. Fortunately, this wasn't too difficult, though the feminist sisters themselves fought against this developing strand of the movement. But Dianic Witchcraft is inherently feminist.

The way I propagated the Dianic Tradition was just pledging to be there every sabbat and esbat; full moons and seasonal celebrations. Gather the women, whoever is coming, and lead the worship of the Goddess on moonlit mountaintops. This promise I fulfilled for ten years. In that decade we had circles from just a dozen women to hundreds of women (much dependent upon the weather!).

The Dianic Tradition was picked up by the lesbian sisters, for whom this was a natural spirituality. I have travelled across the country and danced the spiral dance with women every Halloween and Beltane. In the Dianic tradition the straight women found a refuge; a safe place away from their men. The pure female energy we generated in these circles taught us that we are whole and powerful without the men. Nothing is out of balance. Women are healed.

The first ten years flew by fast. Then came another ten years when I was teaching the teachers. Suddenly we are the fastest growing tradition in the Craft. I am grateful for our expansion. We are not centralized; there is no one leader, no rules or regulations. Can we trust women this much with soul matters?... You bet!

Today we are everywhere. Women-only circles formed in the Christian churches against all the propaganda. Nuns, ex-nuns, creation spirituality Unitarians, gay churches—they all have women-only worship. And then there is a large unmeasurable grass-roots movement. These are the women who practice with their families as of old, or solo, occasionally coming together in workshops and seasonal celebrations.

In all the states throughout the United States there are summer festivals of the Goddess. The Goddess Movement attracted a lot of good press. Female journalists found their voices and wrote supportive articles about the Goddess work. But where the Goddess most visibly triumphed was in publishing. Since the time I wrote the first feminist Witchcraft book in the seventies,* the magical literature has expanded into row upon row of Goddess titles, not just self-published (as was mine) but by major publishers. My latest book, *Goddess in the Office*, is reaching the working woman. The "goddesses" out there are reading and practicing, and finding each other.

The Feminist Book of Lights and Shadows.

From the marginalized and demonized (they celebrate the menstrual bloods) Women's Spirituality Movement has evolved in twenty years into a respected mainstream tradition. There are university Departments of Women's Studies teaching women's spirituality. You can even get a degree in it nowadays.

It is no longer heresy to say that women must gather on their own, without the men, to find their own soul center. Men themselves discovered the same truth, as the fledgling men's movement testifies. As Goddess worship has grown up into a substantial cultural component, I would now like to see the rest of our old/new Goddess culture return. Return and celebrate the theater, the dances, the festivals, the calendar. Celebrating the holy days of the earth we are helping Mother Gaia, our holy mother, to get respect. Celebrating the moons we are helping ourselves, as women, to regain our self-respect. The connections of the cycles of the moon and our menstrual cycle are honored in our practices, not denied or explained away as "a curse"!

There was a lot to discover in the process of growing up as a movement. We discovered how patriarchal religions lied to us about our spiritual heritage; our own divine heritage covered up by lies. It took all kinds of roads to arrive back at the center of our spirit. Women's spirituality is now a mixture of the Old Religion, Jungian psychology, modern feminism, eco-feminism, self-help movement, and self-improvement movement, with a bit of recovery from male-dominated religions thrown in.

Each of us brings our own unique perspective to women's spirituality. In the Dianic Tradition we have no rules for what a woman must or must not do in order to qualify as Dianic, other than that her circle must be all female and that she will not evoke male gods. Therefore some women may have very lively rituals while others may have very sedate ones. I am of the old school of always reaching for ecstasy through improvisations, spontaneous prayers, group movement, and music. But this is really a matter of style. I don't think that our enemies could defeat us, but if our circles go the boring way we can go out of style again.

In order to keep Goddess circles interesting I suggest always to include everybody in the making of prayers, invocations, tending the altar, singing, and power-raising. If only a committee plans the circles they will not be organic. The circles tend to go "down the drain" when conceived in the livingroom, for example, and it doesn't fit the woods or halls where the ritual is going to take place. It's best to plan on the spot where the ritual is to happen.

The Dianic tradition is a teaching tradition. It was custom to entrust the Dianic communities with the instruction of young men and women till a certain age. Young men learned about the natural world and games, but in all-girl groups the girls learned about their womanhood. The boys then were further instructed by Dianic male priests and initiated into manhood, dedicated to this God or that. The girls stayed on and continued the teaching tradition. Sometimes queens of various countries of antiquity took off time and joined a Dianic community — "joined Diana on the mountaintops." We hear about how, upon their return, they would sport gifts from the Goddess, such as an arrow that would never miss, or some other magical article.

The worship of the Earth and her daughter gave role models for human women to interact and appreciate each other. Demeter's lament, when her daughter is kidnapped to Hades, is an all-too-realistic pain for many mothers whose daughters have been raped or murdered. The healing has begun between mothers and daughters...a hopeful sign for our species.

Women's Spirituality is the healing process which is guiding us through the changes at the beginning of the end of patriarchy. So be it!

13: BASIS OF FACT (WITCHES AND FAIRIES)

Amodern idea of a Witch is of someone riding through the air on a broomstick. Witches, of course, never did fly through the air but, as with many of these misconceptions, there is a core of truth to the story. In those early days an old act of fertility was for the villagers to go to the fields in the light of the full moon, taking with them their pitchforks, broomsticks, or just long poles. At the fields they would ride these sticks and poles, like hobbyhorses. They would dance around the fields in the light of the moon, jumping up into the air as they danced. The idea was to show the crops how high to grow! It was a form of *sympathetic* magick. This was typical of the simple, basic form of both the religion and its magick. The religion had developed slowly and naturally, as humankind itself had done.

Incidentally, it is interesting to note that, according to the Church, for a Witch to fly through the air must be the work of the Devil, yet the levitations of such as St. Joseph of Cupertino (seventy flights recorded in the *Acta Sanctorum*) were regarded as miracles! However, as with the broomsticks, so with many other popular ideas: the pointed hat, the cauldron of evil brew!

When the main festivals were held, large numbers of followers of the Old Religion would meet together to celebrate. A number of covens would join together at a pre-arranged spot, usually a large field. The Messenger, also known as "The Messenger of the Gods," would be sent out by the Witch Queen to her various covens to advise them of the details. He (seldom "she," for some reason) would be recognized by the red garters he wore—red silk ribbons tied just below the knees.

Often Witches from the further covens would have to travel some distance to get to the chosen site. Today we might take along a picnic hamper, barbecue, or similar, so that we could have a meal when we got there. In those days it was a case of carrying one large cookpot and driving along chickens, ducks, or geese. At the site local herbs, fruit, and nuts would be gathered, water pulled from the nearby stream, a fire would be built and the poultry would be cooked in the cookpot. This cauldron, then, was simply a campfire cookpot for the end-of-journey meal before the religious festivities began. But from this came the wild stories of "boiling up children at the Sabbat meetings" (where did all these children come from, and how come no one missed them?)!

We know, from Shakespeare and other sources, that the Witches threw into these pots the most gruesome ingredients, right? There were things like the tongue of a snake, bloody fingers, catgut, donkey's eyes, frog's foot, goat's beard, a Jew's ear,

A Witch cutting herbs using a boleen

mouse tail, snake head, swine snout, wolf's foot, and so on. Pretty disgusting by the sound of it—if you take them at face value! For in fact these were all the most innocuous of ingredients; normal plants and herbs.

Today all plants have a Latin name, so that they may be distinct and positively identified. Yet years ago they were known only by common, local names. A plant or herb might be known by one name in one part of the country and a quite different name in another part of the country. And these names were colorful ones, frequently given to the plant because of its looks, color, or other attributes. In the above list, adder's tongue was a name given to the dogtooth violet (*Erythronium americanum*); bloody fingers was the foxglove (*Digitalis purpurea*); catgut was the hoary pea (*Tephrosia virginiana*); donkey's eyes were the seeds of the cowage plant (*Mucuna pruriens*); frog's foot was the bulbous buttercup (*Ranunculus bulbosus*); goat's beard was the vegetable oyster (*Tragopogon porrofolius*); Jew's ear was a fungus that grew on elder trees and elm trees (*Peziza auricula*); mouse tail was common stonecrop (*Sedum acre*); snake head was balmony (*Chelone glabra*); swine snout was the dandelion (*Taraxacum dens leonis*); and wolf's foot was bugle weed (*Lycopus virginicus*). So the seemingly fearsome concoctions that the Witches mixed up in their cauldrons were nothing more than simple herbs going into a cookpot!

Throughout the fifteenth century a popular headdress for women was the tall, conical "dunce's hat," sometimes with a brim but more often without. By the early sixteenth century this was no longer a fashion in court or in the larger cities and towns. The fashion—indeed, the very hats themselves—eventually found its way out to the country, out to the small villages and farms. Part of the purging by the New Religion was to show that the Old Religion was outdated. Witches (and remember that most of them now lived out in the countryside) were therefore pictured, at that time, wearing the demodé headgear. They were shown as "behind the times," as—if I may—"old hat"!

Above I mentioned the foxglove—*Digitalis purpurea*. It is an interesting fact that modern-day doctors will sometimes "discover" something that was common knowledge to the Wica— the "wise ones"—of old. William Withering, an English doctor, isolated an ingredient found in the leaves of the foxglove...*digitalis*, one of the most important of remedies for heart problems. Yet this, as "bloody fingers," had been administered for generations by the Wican herbalists. Dr. Cheney, of Stanford University, "discovered" that raw cabbage juice helped heal stomach ulcers—common knowledge to the Wicans of old.

Why is the Jack-o'-lantern carried at Halloween? Is it meant to be a ghost? And why are ghosts thought of at Halloween? In a way, yes, the pumpkin is a ghost; or rather, a departed spirit. Samhain was the most important of the Witches' festivals. It was the time between the end of the old year and the start of the new, when departed spirits could "slip between the cracks of time" and return to celebrate with their Wica friends and loved ones. As they travelled to the Sabbat, therefore, the Witches carried along a light to symbolize the departed spirit traveling with them. To shield the light, so that it would not be blown out by any wind, it would be carried inside a hollowed out turnip or pumpkin. It was but a step from there to cut out a face, and the Jack-o'-lantern we know today was born.

It was said that when departing for the Sabbat a Witch would leave her cottage by way of the chimney. Certainly by the late Middle Ages* chimneys were of a size that a person could actually climb up or down them, as was done to clean them. But this means of egress was first mentioned by Petrus Mamor, in the fifteenth century (*Flagellum Maleficorum*, Lyons, 1490), and at that time and until the late Middle Ages houses did not have chimneys. Early tradition must therefore refer to exiting via a hole in the roof. This is obviously a carry-over from the times when the majority of common dwellings were built slightly below ground level, with the walls/roof sloping up to a smoke hole at the top. It was then common to enter or exit through the smoke hole. The circular hut excavated at Kestor, in Devon, England, is an excellent example of this type of dwelling, as will be shown later.

---

*The Middle Ages ran from roughly 500 CE to 1500 CE.

In any discussion of Witches there is invariably mention of
fairies. In fact the two are frequently confused. What is the basis
of fact behind the fairy belief?

In every country is found a popular belief in classes of beings
other than humans, inhabiting a region of their own. In the case
of fairies the conception is one of their living inside hills, caverns,
or in water. The belief in fairies is certainly very ancient and
widespread, and the same ideas concerning them are to be found
among uncultivated races as much as in the poesy of more civi-
lized people. Among the Kelts and Teutons the fairies are the
counterparts of mankind in actions, dwellings, enjoyments, and
modes of life. They live in families and societies, some communities being very rich and having magnificent dwellings while
others are poor and beg, borrow, or steal food. The belief is
known in every branch of the Kelts in Ireland, Scotland, the Isle
of Man, Wales, and Brittany, and of the Teutonic races in Scandinavia, Germany, and Britain.

The popular definition of fairies as "little people" is one
which can be quite readily accepted. However, the conception of
such "little people" as tiny beings of aerial and ethereal nature,
able to fly on a bat's back or to sip honey from the flowers
"where the bee sucks," may be regarded as simply the outcome
of imagination working upon a basis of fact. Indeed, if fairies had
ever been such miniature entities it would seem strange that
there was such a widespread fear of them.

The blame for the waning of these beings must be laid at the
doors of Shakespeare and Spenser. After the appearance of the
Faerie Queen, all distinctions were confounded; the names and
attributes of the real Fays, or fairies, of romance were completely
transferred to the little beings who made "the green sour ringlets

whereof the ewe not bites." The change thus effected by the poets established itself firmly among the peoples.

A very close parallel may be found in Yesso, Japan. The dwarfs of this area survived as a separate community until the first half of the seventeenth century, if not later. They were under four feet in height and occupied semi-subterranean or "pit" dwellings. Although the modern inhabitants of that island still describe them, on the whole, in these terms, a new belief regarding them has recently sprung up. The Aino word signifying "pit-dweller" is also not unlike the word for a bur-dock leaf. It was known that the dwarfs were little people; obviously, then (runs the more modern thinking), their name must have meant "people living under burdock leaves" (instead of "in pits")! So, to some of the modern natives of Yesso, those historical dwarfs of the seventeenth century were "so small that if caught in a shower of rain they would shelter under a burdock leaf"!

The Irish word for fairy is *sheehogue* (*sidheog*), a diminutive of "shee" as in *banshee*. The fairies are "the Gods of the Earth," says the Book of Armagh. They were the gods of pagan Ireland—the *Tuatha De Danaan*—whose chief occupations, according to William Butler Yeats (*Irish Fairy and Folk Tales*, New York), were feasting, fighting, making love, and playing the most beautiful of music. In *Popular Tales of the Western Highlands* (1890), J.F. Campbell says:

> I believe there once was a small race of people in these islands, who are remembered as fairies, for the fairy belief is not confined to the Highlanders of Scotland. This class of stories is so widely spread, so matter-of-fact, hangs so well together,

and is so implicitly believed all over the United Kingdom that I am persuaded of the former exis-tence of a race of men in these islands who were smaller in stature than the Celts; who used stone arrows, lived in conical mounds like the Lapps, knew some mechanical arts, pilfered goods and stole children; and were perhaps cotemporary [sic] with some species of wild cattle and horses.

That Campbell was right to believe the fairies "smaller in stature than the Celts," yet not diminutive, can be verified by resorting to historical fact rather than poetic fiction. In Orkney, Jonet Drever was "convict and guilty of the fostering of a bairn in the hill of Westray to the fairy-folk, called on her our good neighbours" (*Maitland Club Miscellany II*, 1840). Master John Walsh consulted with the fairies in Dorset and also "went among the hills" to do it (*Examination of John Walsh*, 1566). Christian Lewingstone, of Leith, said that her daughter was taken away with the fairy-folk. All her herbal and magickal knowledge she got from this same daughter, who "met with the fairy" (*Criminal Trials II*, Pitcairn, 1833) In all of these instances the fairies were of almost the same size as their acquaintances, the humans. Sometimes a mortal would be visited by a fairy and not realize it till sometime after the fairy had gone. Many friend-ships existed between fairy and mortal, and there was even a number of marriages recorded between the two.

Even Shakespeare admits to their true size when, in *The Merry Wives of Windsor*, he has Mistress Anne Page, a full-grown woman, not only dress as a fairy but expect to be accepted as one. In the *Historia de Gentibus Septentrionalibus*, by the Swedish bishop Olaus Magnus (1558) is to be found an illustration of a

A fairy hill

From *Historia de Gentibus Septentrionalibus* by Olaus Magnus, Antwerp, 1558

knight visiting a fairy hill. The fairies in this case are shown as being smaller than the knight, but by no means Lilliputian.

Another pointer to the true size of fairies is the *changeling*. Sometimes the fairies were said to fancy "mortals" and carry them away into their own country, leaving instead some sickly fairy child. Yeats claims that:

> It is on record that once when a mother was leaning over a wizened changeling the latch lifted and a fairy came in, carrying home again the wholesome stolen baby. 'It was the others,' she said, 'who stole it.' As for her, she wanted her own child.

Probably the most acceptable theory regarding the true identity of the "little people" is that they were a people historically known as the *Picts*. The Picts were of the same race as the Lapps, and here are found many similarities. Lapps, Picts, and fairies were all small statured races. The fairies were said to live inside hollow hillocks and under the ground. There yet exist numerous underground structures and artificial mounds whose interior shows them to have been dwelling places, and these are in some places known as "fairy halls" and in others as "Picts' houses."

Fairy herds are often referred to and Campbell suggests that certain of these, in Sutherlandshire for example, were probably reindeer, which the "fairies" milked. Reindeer were hunted in that part of Scotland as recently as the twelfth century. Remains of reindeer horns are still to be found in the counties of Sutherland, Ross, and Caithness, sometimes in the very structures ascribed to the Picts.

The Lapp-Dwarf parallel was gone into fully by Professor Nilsson, in his *Primitive Inhabitants of Scandinavia*, in 1870. Sir Walter Scott referred to it and accepted it. "There seems reason to conclude," Nilsson says, "that these *duergar* (in English, "dwarfs") were originally nothing else than the diminutive natives of the Lappish, Lettish and Finnish nations who, flying before the conquering weapons of the Asae, sought the most retired regions of the north and there endeavored to hide themselves from their eastern invaders."

Strabo is the only writer of antiquity who questions the existence of dwarfs. All the others are on the side of Aristotle, who says: "This is no fable; there really exists in that region (the sources of the Nile), as people relate, a race of little men, who have small horses and live in holes." Pliny and other writers speak of dwarf tribes in other localities, and among these are "the vague regions of the north, designated by the name Thule." This area, vague enough certainly, is the territory with which the Picts are associated; as also, of course, the fairies of North European tradition.

The attributes with which the little people of North Europe are accredited cannot be given in detail here. It is enough to note that they were believed to live in houses wholly or partly underground (the latter kind being described as "hollow" mounds or hills) and that when people of a taller race entered such subterranean dwellings they found the domestic utensils of the dwarfs were of the kind labeled "prehistoric." The copper vessels, which dwarf women sometimes left behind them when discovered surreptitiously milking the cows of their neighbors, were likewise of an antique form. They helped themselves to the beef and mutton of their neighbors, after having shot the animals with flint-headed arrows. Many families in many districts are believed to have inherited some of their blood. Of this intercourse between the taller races and the dwarfs there are many records in the old traditions. In the days when, as Chaucer tells, the land was "ful-filled of faerie," the knights errant had usually a dwarf as an attendant. According to Highland tradition every high-caste family of pure Gaelic descent had an attendant dwarf. These examples show the "little people" in a not unfriendly light. But many other stories speak of them as "malignant foes" and as dreaded oppressors.

In Highland Scotland fairies were called *daoine sithe*, or "men of peace." Scottish fairy folklore resembles that of Ireland, though of a more sombre cast. In Ireland, where the belief is strongest, the fairies are called "good people," and are of a benevolent but capricious and mischievous disposition. The Fairy Mistress of Ireland (*Leanhaun Shee*) seeks the love of mortals. Yeats relates that if they refuse her love she must be their slave, but if they consent they are hers and can only escape by finding another to take their place. The Fairy Mistress of Scotland (*Cannan sith*) compelled her lover to hold nightly assignations, and gave him wonderful information—being strongly reminiscent of Numa and the nymph Egeria, with whom he held nightly meetings and who gave him divine knowledge.

An Irish manuscript of the eleventh or twelfth century (*The War of the Gaedhil with the Gail*) states that when the ninth century Danes overran and plundered Ireland there was nothing "in concealment under ground in Errin, or in the various secret places belonging to the fairies" that they did not discover and appropriate. This statement receives confirmation from a Scandinavian record, the *Landnama-bok*, which says that in or about the year 870 a well-known Norse chief named Lief "went on warfare in the west. He made war in Ireland and there found a large underground house; he went down into it, and it was dark until a light shone from a sword in the hand of a man. Lief killed the man, and took the sword and much property...He made war widely in Ireland and got much property."

The earliest alleged reference to the Picts which shows them akin to the fairies is placed in the middle of the fifteenth century, before the Orkney Islands had passed from the Crown of Denmark to the Crown of Scotland. A manuscript of the then Bishop of Orkney, dated Kirwall 1443, states that when Harald Haarfagr conquered the Orkneys, in the ninth century, the inhabitants were the two nations of the *Papae* and the *Peti*, both of whom were exterminated. The *Peti* were certainly the *Pehts*, or Picts. Of these Picts of Orkney it is said that they "were only a little exceeding pygmies in stature and worked wonderfully in the construction of their cities, evening and morning, but in the midday, being quite destitute of strength, they hid themselves in little houses underground." The exact date of this statement is unknown but it is quite in accordance with the widespread ideas held throughout Scotland and Northumberland with regard to the Picts: that they were great as builders but were of very low stature and closely akin to the fairies. They were famous for doing their work at night and, whatever the explanation for the above curious statement that at midday they lost their strength and withdrew to their underground houses,* it is interesting to compare it with the remark made by the traveller Pennant as he was passing along Glenorchy in 1772 (*Voyages: Second Tour of Scotland*, 1809). The entry in his journal reads:

> See frequently on the road-sides small verdant hillocks styled by the common people "shi an" (*sithean*), or the fairy-haunt, because here, say they, the fairies, who love not the glare of day, make their retreat after the celebration of their nocturnal revels.

As the "Picts' houses" are, to outward appearance, "small verdant hillocks," the parallel is very exact.

Yeats, in *Irish Fairy and Folk Tales*, relates that:

> Forts, otherwise raths or royalties, are circular ditches enclosing a little field where, if you dig down, you come to stone chambers, their beehive roofs and walls made of unmortared stone. In

---

* Could this be a *siesta*, of the South American and Mediterranean variety, where everyone stops work in the middle of the day and retires to their homes to sleep and rest?

these little fields the ancient Celts fortified themselves and their cattle, in winter retreating into the
stone chambers, where also they were buried.

The various Hebridean structures associated with the Picts
are commonly spoken of as beehive houses, but their Gaelic
name is *bo'h* or *bothan*. They are now only used as temporary res-
idences or "shealings" by those who herd cattle at their summer
pasturage, but at one time were the permanent dwellings of the
people. Sir Arthur Mitchell, in *The Past in the Present*, thus
describes his first sight of the beehive houses:

> By the side of the burn which flowed through a
> long grassy glen we saw two small round hive-like
> hillocks, not much higher than a man, joined
> together, and covered with grass and weeds. Out of
> the top of one of them a column of smoke slowly
> rose, and at its base there was a hole about three
> feet high and two feet wide, which seemed to lead
> into the interior of the hillock—its hollowness,
> and the possibility of its having a human creature
> within it being thus suggested. There was no one,
> however, actually within the *bo'h* when we came in
> sight; the three girls being seated on a knoll by the
> burnside, but it was really in the inside of these
> two green hillocks that they slept, cooked their
> food, carried on their work and, in short, dwelt.

The walls, built of rough stone without any mortar, were
very thick and were covered, on the outside, with turf which
soon became grassy like the land round about, and thus secured
perfect wind and water tightness.

Circular hut, of the type found at Kestor, Devon, England

Of another much larger such dwelling, with several entrances, Sir Arthur observes "it could have accommodated from forty to fifty people." To this larger class the term "earth house" is most frequently accorded in Scotland, though the term *weem* is also used. This is merely a quickened pronunciation of the Gaelic *uam* (or *uamb*), a cave, and it is a reminder that in both Gaelic and English the word "cave" is by no means restricted to a natural cavity. One such artificial structure is known as *Uamb Sgalabhad*, the "Cave of Sgalabhad." Another Gaelic name for these underground galleries is *tigh fo thalaimh*, or "house beneath the ground."

As has been mentioned, at Kestor, in Devon, England, is to be found a fairy house or hill. It is a circular hut dating from the Bronze Age (circa 400 BCE). Thirty-seven feet in diameter, and circular in plan, it is sunk two or three feet into the earth. The lower, sunken, walls are lined with stones; the upper part was of wattle-and-daub or of turf. The roof was supported by posts carrying a wooden frame. In the middle of the hut was the hearth, and there was a small opening in the roof to allow the smoke to escape. Outwardly such a house had all the appearance of a natural hill. One of the inhabitants, a "look-out," would sit on the center of the roof, entering and leaving by way of the smoke hole, as has been mentioned. Such a building may well have been the "green chapel"—a huge grassy mound with a concealed entrance—mentioned in the fourteenth century romance *Sir Gawain and the Green Knight*. Green, of course, is by tradition the favorite color of both fairies and Witches.

The fairies frequented many parts of the Bishopric of Durham, in England. There is a hillock, or *tumulus*, near Bishopton, and a large hill near Billingham, both of which used to be "haunted by fairies" according to local tradition. Even *Ferry-Hill*, between Darlington and Durham, is evidently a corruption of *Fairy-Hill*.

In Irish folklore is found the Pooka (*Puca*), who possibly derives his name from *poc*, a he-goat. He is said to live on solitary mountains and hills. An old manuscript story (*Mac-na-Michombairle*, c. 12th C.) tells that:

> Out of a certain hill in Leinster there used to emerge as far as his middle a plump, sleek, terrible, steed and speak in human voice to each person about November-day*, and he was accustomed to give intelligent and proper answers to such as consulted him concerning all that would befall them until the November of next year. And the people used to leave gifts and presents at the hill.

---

*Probably Samhain.

Obviously the inhabitant of a fairy hill serving as the local oracle, wearing the mask of a horse which, from the brief description, sounds not unlike the jackal mask worn by Egyptian priests at Denderah or the Dorset *Oozer*, once familiar in the west of England. From the *Leabhar Sgeulaigheachia* also comes the story of a Pooka who, late one night, takes a piper to play at "a great feast in the house of the Banshee, on top of the Croagh Patric." The house of the Banshee turns out to be the hill Croagh Patric itself, or the top of it, and when the Pooka "struck three blows with his foot a great door opened and they passed together into a fine room."

Some of the Scottish hill-dwellings are still inhabited for months at a time, though their inhabitants are not now fairies. But it is among those people that stories of fairies are most rife, and many claim an actual descent from them. Although they are certainly not pygmies, yet they live in a district in which the *small* type of that heterogeneous nation is still quite discernable, and that part of the island of Lewis (*Uig*) which has longest retained those places as dwellings is inhabited by a caste whom other Hebrideans describe as small and regard as different from themselves. A study of the dimensions of the oldest structures will show that they could not have been built or inhabited by any but a race of actual dwarfs, as tradition says they were. The Little People; the Fairies.

What of other beliefs and practices frequently termed "witchcraft"? The Pennsylvania Dutch—those people who live in southern Pennsylvania, between the Delaware and the Susquehanna Rivers—have a belief in what they call "witchcraft" or *hexerie*. Basically an extremely religious people, they are also notoriously superstitious. They believe, for example, that a cross painted on a door handle will prevent the Devil from entering.

From such simple beliefs came the beautiful, extremely colorful "hex" signs found in that part of the country. They are usually found fastened to the sides of barns. They are not used by the Amish and Mennonites—the plain sects—but by the Lutherans, Reformed, and other church people.

Different designs are used for different things. For good luck, success, and happiness, a hex symbol of the triple star is used. For sun and rain, for crop abundance and water, a four-pointed star enclosing a five-pointed star within a circle, together with four teardrops. For faith in yourself, in what you do, and in your fellow man, the double *Distelfink* (the Distelfink is a bird, much like a goldfinch, which uses thistledown for its nest).

There is a wealth of superstition in this area. For instance, if a black cat crosses your path it means bad luck, and the only way it can be negated is by seeing a white horse and a red-headed woman! Such is the "witchcraft," so called, of Pennsylvania.

Many primitive peoples are accused of "witchcraft" by the Christians. Christian missionaries were (are?) always quick to tag anything with which they were unfamiliar as "witchcraft." If they encountered a people previously unadulterated by modern "civilization," they would automatically label them as "devil-worshippers" and their practices as "witchcraft." The deities might be totally benign and the morals of the people without fault but, just because they had never heard of Jesus, the missionaries would insist on "saving" them and, in doing so, destroying their culture. The so-called "witchcraft" of such peoples is not necessarily the same as that which we have examined in this book. Undoubtedly there would be parallels, for these people are certainly Pagans, but there would probably not be the same celebration of the eight festivals of the year nor the hierarchy of covens. "Witchcraft," when applied to African and other primitive peoples, is generally a misnomer of the Christians.

True Witchcraft, or Wica, as we have seen in this book, is a living, positive religion that is growing rapidly as more and more people learn the truth about it. It is a viable alternative to many of the long established religions such as Christianity, Buddhism, and Judaism. It is, at last, regaining its rightful place as a religion of the people—Wica, the Old Religion: the Craft of the Wise.

BIBLIOGRAPHY

There have been hundreds, if not thousands, of books written about Witchcraft. As has been shown, most of them have been from the very perverted Christian point of view. Only in recent years have we had the Witches' own side of the story presented. Here, first, are some of the really worthwhile books on the Old Religion that should be read by everyone sincerely interested in the Craft.

Bracelin, J.L. *Gerald Gardner: Witch*. London: Octagon Press, 1960.

Branston, B. *Lost Gods of England*. London: Thames and Hudson, 1957.

Buckland, R. *Buckland's Complete Book of Witchcraft*. St. Paul, MN: Llewellyn, 1986.

—————. *Scottish Witchcraft*. St. Paul, MN: Llewellyn, 1991.

—————. *The Tree: Complete Book of Saxon Witchcraft*. York Beach, ME: Weiser, 1974.

Crowther, P. and A. *The Witches Speak*.

Cunningham, S. *Wicca*. St. Paul, MN: Llewellyn, 1988.

—————. *Living Wicca*. St. Paul, MN: Llewellyn, 1993.

Farrar, Stewart and Janet. *What Witches Do*. London: Coward, McCann, 1971.

—————. *Eight Sabbats For Witches*. London: Hale, 1981.

—————. *The Witches' Way*. London: Hale, 1985.

Farren, D. *The Return of Magic*. New York: Harper & Row, 1973.

Gardner, G.B. (pseudonym "Scire"). *High Magic's Aid*. London: Houghton, 1949 (novel).

—————. *Witchcraft Today*. London: Rider, 1954.

—————. *The Meaning of Witchcraft*. London: Aquarian Press, 1959.

Graves, R. *The White Goddess*, London: 1948.

Guiley, R.E. *The Encyclopedia of Witches and Witchcraft*. New York: Facts on File, 1992.

Kenyan, T. *Witches Still Live*. 1928.

Leland, C.G. *Aradia: Gospel of the Witches of Italy*. London: Nutt, 1899.

Lethbridge, T.C. *Witches*. London: Routledge & Kegan Paul, 1962.

Murray, M.A. *The Witch-Cult in Western Europe*. London: Oxford University Press, 1921.

——————. *God of the Witches*. London: Sampson Low Marston, 1931.

Starkey, M. *The Devil in Massachusetts*. New York: Knopf, 1949.

Valiente, D. *Where Witchcraft Lives*. London: Aquarian Press, 1962.

——————. *An ABC of Witchcraft Past and Present*. New York: St. Martins, 1973.

——————. *Witchcraft for Tomorrow*. New York: St. Martin's, 1978.

——————. *The Rebirth of Witchcraft*. London: Hale, 1989.

Hereunder are listed those books that have been mentioned in the text, together with other volumes which are also of interest to the general study of the subject.

Ady, T. *A Candle in the Dark*. London: 1656.

Alford, V. "The Abbots Bromley Horn Dance." *Antiquity*, June 1933.

Anwyl, E. *Celtic Religion in Pre-Christian Times*. London: 1906.

Baroja, J.C. *The World of Witches*. London: 1964.

Bede. *Ecclesiastical History of the English Nation*. n.d.

Bord, J. and C. *Earth Rites*. London: 1982.

——————. *Ancient Mysteries of Britain*. London: Guild Publishing, 1986.

Borromeo, Sr. M.C. *The New Nuns.* New York: NAL, 1967.

Bowra, C.M. *Primitive Song.* New York: World Publishing, 1962.

Breasted, J.H. *Development of Religion and Thought in Ancient Egypt.* New York: Harper, 1960.

Budapest, Z. *The Holy Book of Women's Mysteries.* 1983.

——————. *The Grandmother of Time.* 1989.

——————. *Grandmother Moon.*

——————. *Goddess in the Office.* 1993.

Budge, Sir E.A.W. *Amulets and Talismans.* New York: University Books, 1961.

——————. *Egyptian Magic.* London: 1899.

Burland, C.A. *The Magical Arts.* New York: Horizon, 1966.

——————. *Echoes of Magic.* London: Davies, 1972.

Burr, G.L. *Narratives of the Witchcraft Cases 1648–1706.* New York: Barnes & Noble, 1914.

Caesar, J. *Gallic Wars.* Oxford: Loeb, 1917.

Campanelli, P. *Ancient Ways.* St. Paul, MN: Llewellyn, 1991.

——————. *Wheel of the Year.* St. Paul, MN: Llewellyn, 1989.

Campanelli, P. and D. *Circles, Groves and Sanctuaries.* St. Paul, MN: Llewellyn, 1992.

Campbell, J. *Popular Tales of the Western Highlands.* Edinburgh: 1890.

——————. *Witchcraft and Second Sight in the Highlands and Islands of Scotland.* Edinburgh: 1902.

Chadwick, N.K. *Celtic Britain.* New York: Praeger, 1963.

DeGivry, G. *A Pictorial Anthology of Witchcraft, Magic and Alchemy.* New York: University Books, 1958.

Eliade, M. *Rites and Symbols of Initiation—Birth and Rebirth.* New York: Harper, 1958.

—————. *Patterns in Comparative Religion.* New York: 1958.

Fitch, E. *Magical Rites from the Crystal Well.* St. Paul, MN: Llewellyn, 1983.

—————. *Rites of Odin.* St. Paul, MN: Llewellyn, 1992.

Fletcher, R. *The Witches' Pharmacopoeia.* Proceedings of the Historical Club of the Johns Hopkins Hospital, April 13, 1896.

Fortescue, Sir J. *In Praise of the Laws of England.* London: 1468.

Foxcroft, H.C. "On Witches' Sabbaths." *Quest* 14, 1923, p. 209.

Frazer, J.G. *The Golden Bough.* London: 1890.

—————. *The Worship of Nature.* London: 1926.

Freud, S. *Totem and Taboo.* Trans. J. Strachey. New York: Norton, 1952.

Glanvill, J. *Sadducismus Triumphatus.* London, 1681.

Glass, J. *Witchcraft, the Sixth Sense and Us.*

Goldberg, P.Z. *The Sacred Fire.* New York: Horace Liveright, 1930.

Hassal, W.O. *They Saw It Happen.* Oxford: Blackwell, 1957.

Hawkes, J. *History in Earth and Stone.* Harvard U.P., 1952.

Heckethorn, C.W. *Secret Societies of All Ages and Countries.* New York: University Books, 1965.

Hill, D., and P. Williams. *The Supernatural.* New York: Hawthorn, 1966.

Hole, C. *Witchcraft in England.* New York: Scribners, 1947.

—————. *A Mirror of Witchcraft.* London: Chatto and Windus, 1957.

Hughes, P. *Witchcraft.* London: Longmans Green, 1952.

Huxley, A. *The Evolution of Theology*—"Science and Hebrew Tradition."

James, E.O. *The Ancient Gods.* New York: Putnam, 1960.

James I, King. *Demonologie.* Edinburgh, 1597.

Jevons, F.B. *An Introduction to the History of Religion.* London: 1896.

Kavanaugh, Fr. J.*A Modern Priest Looks At His Outdated Church.* New York: Trident, 1967.

Kelly, A. *Crafting the Art of Magic, Vol. I.* St. Paul, MN: Llewellyn, 1991.

Kittredge, G.L. *Witchcraft in Old and New England.* New York: Russell & Russell, 1956.

Larousse. *Larousse Encyclopedia of Mythology.* London: Hamlyn, 1959.

Lethbridge, T.C. *Gogmagog—The Buried Gods.* London: Routledge Kegan Paul, 1957.

Loher, H. *Hochnotige unterhanige wemutige Klage der frommen Unschultigen.* Germany: 1676.

Macalister, R.A. *The Archaeology of Ireland.* London: 1928.

Mamor, P. *Flagellum Maleficorum.* Lyons: 1490.

Maple, E. *The Dark World of Witches.* London: Hale, 1962.

Martello, L. *Witchcraft: The Old Religion.* New Jersey: University Books, 1974.

Mather, C. *Memorable Provinces Relating to Witchcraft and Possessions.* Boston: 1689.

—————. *Wonders of the Invisible World.* Boston: 1693.

McCoy, E. *Witta: An Irish Pagan Tradition.* St. Paul, MN: Llewellyn, 1993.

—————. *A Witch's Guide to Faery Folk.* St. Paul, MN: Llewellyn, 1994.

Melton, J.G. *Encyclopedia of American Religions.* Chicago: Gale Research, 1983.

Michelet, J. *Satanism and Witchcraft.* London: Arco, 1958.

Morganwg, I. *Barddas.* Llandovery: 1862.

Murray, M.A. "Organizations of Witches in Great Britain." *Folklore* 28, 1917.

—————. "Witches and the Number 13." *Folklore* 31, 1920.

Nilsson, Prof. *Primitive Inhabitants of Scandinavia.* 1870.

Notestein, W. *A History of Witchcraft in England from 1558 to 1718.* New York: Russell & Russell, 1965.

O'Gaea, A. *The Family Wicca Book.* St. Paul, MN: Llewellyn, 1993.

Peel, E., and P. Southern. *The Trials of the Lancashire Witches.* New York, 1969.

Persson, A.W. *The Religion of Greece in Prehistoric Times*. University of California Press, 1942.

Pitcairn, R. *Criminal Trials*. Edinburgh: 1833.

Randolph, V. *Ozark Superstitions*. Columbia University Press, 1947.

Rhodes, H.T.F. *The Satanic Mass*. London: Rider, 1954.

Ritson, J. *Fairy Tales Now First Collected*. London: 1831.

Robbins, R.H. *The Encyclopedia of Witchcraft and Demonology*. New York: Crown, 1965.

Rymer, T. *Foedera*. London: 1704.

Scot, R. *Discoverie of Witchcraft*. London: 1584.

Scott, Sir W. *Demonology and Witchcraft*. London: Harper's Family Library No. XI, 1831.

Seth, R. *Children Against Witches*. New York: 1969.

Shah, I. *The Secret Lore of Magic*. New York: Citadel, 1958.

Sjoestedt, M-L. *Gods and Heroes of the Celts*. London: Methuen, 1949.

Sprenger, J., and H.I. Kramer. *Malleus Maleficarum*. Rome: 1486.

Steiger, B. *Sex and Satanism*. New York: Ace, 1969.

Stubbs, W. *Anatomy of Abuses*. London: n.d.

Spence, L. *An Encyclopedia of Occultism*. London: Routledge, 1920.

—————. *The Magic Arts of Celtic Britain*. London: Rider, n.d.

St. Clair, M. *Sign of the Labrys*. New York: Bantam Books, 1963 (novel).

Starhawk (i.e, M. Simos). *Spiral Dance*. New York: Harper & Row, 1979.

Stearne, J. *A Confirmation and Discovery of Witchcraft*. London: 1648.

Stevenson. *Chronicles of Lanercost*. Glasgow: 1839.

St. Leger-Gordon, R.E. *The Witchcraft and Folklore of Dartmoor*. London: Hale, 1965.

Teare, T.G.D. *Folk Doctor's Island*. Athol, IOM, 1963.

Van Gennep, A. *The Rites of Passage*. University of Chicago Press, n.d.

Vitalis, O. *Ecclesiastical History*. London: Bohn, 1847.

Walsh. *Examination of John Walsh*. London: 1566.

Wilde, Lady J. *Ancient Cures, Charms and Usages of Ireland*. London: Ward & Downey, 1890.

Williams, C. *Witchcraft*. London: Faber & Faber, 1941.

Williams, J. *The Witches*. New York: Random House, 1957 (novel).

Yeats, W.B., ed. *Irish Fairy and Folk Tales*. New York: Modern Library No. 44.

INDEX

STAY IN TOUCH

On the following pages you will find listed, with their current prices, some of the books now available on related subjects. Your book dealer stocks most of these and will stock new titles in the Llewellyn series as they become available. We urge your patronage.

To obtain our full catalog, to keep informed about new titles as they are released and to benefit from informative articles and helpful news, you are invited to write for our bimonthly news magazine/catalog, *Llewellyn's New Worlds of Mind and Spirit*. A sample copy is free, and it will continue coming to you at no cost as long as you are an active mail customer. Or you may subscribe for just $10.00 in U.S.A. and Canada ($20.00 overseas, first class mail). Many bookstores also have *New Worlds* available to their customers. Ask for it.

Stay in touch! In *New Worlds'* pages you will find news and features about new books, tapes and services, announcements of meetings and seminars, articles helpful to our readers, news of authors, products and services, special money-making opportunities, and much more.

Llewellyn's New Worlds of Mind and Spirit
P.O. Box 64383-K101, St. Paul, MN 55164-0383, U.S.A.
* * *

TO ORDER BOOKS AND TAPES

If your book dealer does not have the books described on the following pages readily available, you may order them direct from the publisher by sending full price in U.S. funds, plus $3.00 for postage and handling for orders *under* $10.00; $4.00 for orders *over* $10.00. There are no postage and handling charges for orders over $50.00. Postage and handling rates are subject to change. UPS Delivery: We ship UPS whenever possible. Delivery guaranteed. Provide your street address as UPS does not deliver to P.O. Boxes. UPS to Canada requires a $50.00 minimum order. Allow 4-6 weeks for delivery. Orders outside the U.S.A. and Canada: Airmail—add retail price of book; add $5.00 for each non-book item (tapes, etc.); add $1.00 per item for surface mail.

FOR GROUP STUDY AND PURCHASE

Because there is a great deal of interest in group discussion and study of the subject matter of this book, we feel that we should encourage the adoption and use of this particular book by such groups by offering a special quantity price to group leaders or agents.

Our Special Quantity Price for a minimum order of five copies of *Witchcraft from the Inside* is $38.85 cash-with-order. This price includes postage and handling within the United States. Minnesota residents must add 6.5% sales tax. For additional quantities, please order in multiples of five. For Canadian and foreign orders, add postage and handling charges as above. Credit card (VISA, MasterCard, American Express) orders are accepted. Charge card orders only may be phoned in free within the U.S.A. or Canada by dialing 1-800-THE-MOON. For customer service, call 1-612-291-1970. Mail orders to:

LLEWELLYN PUBLICATIONS
P.O. Box 64383-K101, St. Paul, MN 55164-0383, U.S.A.

BUCKLAND'S COMPLETE BOOK OF WITCHCRAFT
by Raymond Buckland

Here is the most complete resource to the study and practice of modern, non-denominational Wicca. This is a lavishly illustrated, self-study course for the solitary or group. Included are rituals; exercises for developing psychic talents; information on all major "sects" of the Craft; sections on tools, beliefs, dreams, meditations, divination, herbal lore, healing, ritual clothing and much, much more. This book unites theory and practice into a comprehensive course designed to help you develop into a practicing Witch, one of the "Wise Ones." It is written by Ray Buckland, a very famous and respected authority on Witchcraft who first came public with the Old Religion in the United States. Large format with workbook-type exercises, profusely illustrated and full of music and chants. Takes you from A to Z in the study of Witchcraft.

Never before has so much information on the Craft of the Wise been collected in one place. Traditionally, there are three degrees of advancement in most Wiccan traditions. When you have completed studying this book, you will be the equivalent of a Third-Degree Witch. Even those who have practiced Wicca for years find useful information in this book, and many covens are using this for their textbook. If you want to become a Witch, or if you merely want to find out what Witchcraft is really about, you will find no better book than this.

0-87542-050-8, 272 pgs., 8 1/2 x 11, illus., softcover $14.95

THE COMMITTEE
by Raymond Buckland

"Duncan's eyes were glued to the destruct button. He saw that the colonel's hand never did get to it. Yet, even as he watched, he saw the red button move downwards, apparently of its own volition. The rocket blew into a million pieces, and the button came back up. No one, Duncan would swear, had physically touched the button, yet it had been depressed."

The Cold War is back in this psi-techno suspense thriller where international aggressors use psychokinesis, astral projection and other psychic means to circumvent the U.S. intelligence network. When two routine communications satellite launches are inexplicably aborted at Vandenberg Air Force Base in California, one senator suspects paranormal influences. He calls in a writer, two parapsychologists and a psychic housewife—and The Committee is formed. Together, they piece together a sinister occult plot against the United States. The Committee then embarks on a supernatural adventure of a lifetime as they attempt to beat the enemy at its own game.

Llewellyn Psi-Fi Fiction Series
1-56718-100-7, 240 pgs., mass market $4.99

DOORS TO OTHER WORLDS
A Practical Guide to Communicating with Spirits
by Raymond Buckland

There has been a revival of spiritualism in recent years, with more and more people attempting to communicate with disembodied spirits via talking boards, séances, and all forms of mediumship (e.g., allowing another spirit to make use of your vocal chords, hand muscles, etc., while you remain in control of your body). The movement, which began in 1848 with the Fox sisters of New York, has attracted the likes of Abraham Lincoln and Queen Victoria, and even blossomed into a full-scale religion with regular services of hymns, prayers, Bible-reading and sermons along with spirit communication.

Doors to Other Worlds is for *anyone* who wishes to communicate with spirits, as well as for the less adventurous who simply wish to satisfy their curiosity about the subject. Explore the nature of the Spiritual Body, learn how to prepare yourself to become a medium, experience for yourself the trance state, clairvoyance, psychometry, table tipping and levitation, talking boards, automatic writing, spiritual photography, spiritual healing, distant healing, channeling, development circles, and also learn how to avoid spiritual fraud.

0-87542-061-3, 272 pgs., 5¼ x 8, illus., softcover $10.00

PRACTICAL CANDLEBURNING RITUALS
Spells & Rituals for Every Purpose
by Raymond Buckland, Ph.D.

Magick is a way in which to apply the full range of your hidden psychic powers to the problems we all face in daily life. We know that normally we use only 5 per cent of our total powers. Magick taps powers from deep inside our psyche where we are in contact with the Universe's limitless resources.

Magick need not be complex—it can be as simple as using a few candles to focus your mind, a simple ritual to give direction to your desire, a few words to give expression to your wish.

This book shows you how easy it can be. Here is Magick for fun, Magick as a Craft, Magick for Success. Love, Luck, Money, Marriage, Healing; Magick to stop slander, to learn truth, to heal an unhappy marriage, to overcome a bad habit, to break up a love affair, etc.

Magick—with nothing fancier than ordinary candles, and the 28 rituals in this book (given in both Christian and Old Religion versions)—can transform your life.

0-87542-048-6, 208 pgs., 5¼ x 8, illus., softcover $6.95

Prices subject to change without notice.

PRACTICAL COLOR MAGICK
by Raymond Buckland, Ph.D.

Color magick is powerful—and safe. Here is a sourcebook for the psychic influence of color on our physical lives. Contains complete rituals and meditations for practical applications of color magick for health, success and love. Find full instructions on how to meditate more effectively and use color to stimulate the chakras and unfold psychic abilities. Learn to use color in divination and in the making of talismans, sigils and magick squares.

This book will teach all the powers of light and more. You'll learn new forms of expression of your innermost self, new ways of relating to others with the secret languages of light and color. Put true color back into your life with the rich spectrum of ideas and practical magical formulas from *Practical Color Magick!*

0-87542-047-8, 160 pgs., 5¼ x 8, illus., softcover $6.95

SCOTTISH WITCHCRAFT
The History & Magick of the Picts
by Raymond Buckland

From the ancient misty Highlands of Scotland to modern-day America come the secrets of solitary Witchcraft practice. *Scottish Witchcraft* explores "PectiWita," or the craft of the Picts, the mysterious early Keltic people. The Scottish PectiWita tradition differs in many ways from the Wicca of England—there is little emphasis on the worship of the gods (though it is there), but more on the living and blending of magick into everyday life.

Many people attracted to modern-day Wicca are unable to contact or join a coven. PectiWita is a path for the solitary Witch; and here, for the first time, are full details of this solitary branch of the Old Ways. Learn the history of the Picts, their origins and beliefs. Learn how to make simple tools and use them to work magic. Through step-by-step instructions you are brought into touch and then into complete harmony with all of nature. Explore their celebrations, talismans, song and dance, herbal lore, runes and glyphs, and recipes. Learn how to practice the religion in the city and with groups. Ray Buckland's contact with the late Aidan Breac, a descendent of the Picts, led to his interest in Scottish Witchcraft and to writing this present volume.

0-87542-057-5, 256 pgs., 5¼ x 8, illus., photos, softcover $9.95

Prices subject to change without notice.

SECRETS OF GYPSY FORTUNETELLING
by Ray Buckland

This book unveils the Romani secrets of fortunetelling, explaining in detail the many different methods used by these nomads. For generations they have survived on their skills as seers. Their accuracy is legendary. They are a people who seem to be born with "the sight" ... the ability to look into the past, present and future using only the simplest of tools to aid them. Here you will learn to read palms, to interpret the symbols in a teacup, to read cards ... both the Tarot and regular playing cards. Here are revealed the secrets of interpreting the actions of animals, of reading the weather, of recognizing birthmarks and the shape of hands. Impress your friends with your knowledge of many of these lesser Mysteries, uncommon forms of fortunetelling known only to a few.

The methods of divination presented in this book are all practical methods—no expensive or hard-to-get items are necessary. The Gypsies are accomplished at using natural objects and everyday items to serve them in their endeavors: Sticks and stones, knives and needles, cards and dice. Using these non-complex objects, and following the traditional Gypsy ways shown, you can become a seer and improve the quality of your own life and of these lives around you.

0-87542-051-6, 240 pgs., mass market, illus. $3.95

SECRETS OF GYPSY LOVE MAGICK
by Raymond Buckland, Ph.D.

One of the most compelling forms of magick—perhaps the most sought after—is love magick. It is a positive form of working, a way to true delight and pleasure. The Gypsies have long been known for the successful working of love magick.

In this book you will find magicks for those who are courting, who are newlyweds, and love magick for the family unit. There is also a section on Gypsy love potions, talismans and amulets.

Included are spells and charms to discover your future spouse, to make your lover your best friend and to bring love into a loveless marriage. You will learn traditional secrets gathered from English Gypsies that are presented here for the first time ever by a Gypsy of Romani blood.

0-87542-053-2, 176 pgs., mass market, illus. $4.99

WICCA
A Guide for the Solitary Practitioner
by Scott Cunningham

Wicca is a book of life, and how to live magically, spiritually, and wholly attuned with Nature. It is a book of sense and common sense, not only about Magick, but about religion and one of the most critical issues of today: how to achieve the much needed and wholesome relationship with out Earth. Cunningham presents Wicca as it is today: a gentle, Earth-oriented religion dedicated to the Goddess and God. This book fulfills a need for a practical guide to solitary Wicca—a need which no previous book has fulfilled.

Here is a positive, practical introduction to the religion of Wicca, designed so that any interested person can learn to practice the religion alone, anywhere in the world. It presents Wicca honestly and clearly, without the pseudo-history that permeates other books. It shows that Wicca is a vital, satisfying part of twentieth century life.

This book presents the theory and practice of Wicca from an individual's perspective. The section on the Standing Stones Book of Shadows contains solitary rituals for the Esbats and Sabbats. This book, based on the author's nearly two decades of Wiccan practice, presents an eclectic picture of various aspects of this religion. Exercises designed to develop magical proficiency, a self-dedication ritual, herb, crystal and rune magic, recipes for Sabbat feasts, are included in this excellent book.

0-87542-118-0, 240 pgs., 6 x 9, illus., softcover $9.95

LIVING WICCA
A Further Guide for the Solitary Practitioner
Scott Cunningham

Living Wicca is the long-awaited sequel to Scott Cunningham's wildly successful *Wicca: a Guide for the Solitary Practitioner.* This new book is for those who have made the conscious decision to bring their Wiccan spirituality into their everyday lives. It provides solitary practitioners with the tools and added insights that will enable them to blaze their own spiritual paths—to become their own high priests and priestesses.

Living Wicca takes a philosophical look at the questions, practices, and differences within Witchcraft. It covers the various tools of learning available to the practitioner, the importance of secrecy in one's practice, guidelines to performing ritual when ill, magical names, initiation, and the Mysteries. It discusses the benefits of daily prayer and meditation, making offerings to the gods, how to develop a prayerful attitude, and how to perform Wiccan rites when away from home or in emergency situations.

Unlike any other book on the subject, *Living Wicca* is a step-by-step guide to creating your own Wiccan tradition and personal vision of the gods, designing your personal ritual and symbols, developing your own book of shadows, and truly living your Craft.

0-87542-184-9, 208 pgs., 6 x 9, illus., softcover $12.95

Prices subject to change without notice.

EARTH POWER
Techniques of Natural Magic
by Scott Cunningham

Magick is the art of working with the forces of Nature to bring about necessar and desired, changes. The forces of Nature—expressed through Earth, Air, Fire and Water—are our "spiritual ancestors" who paved the way for our emergence from the prehistoric seas of creation. Attuning to and working with these energies in magick not only lends you the power to affect changes in your life, it also allows you to sense your own place in the larger scheme of Nature. Using the "Old Ways" enables you to live a better life and to deepen your understanding of the world. The tools and powers of magick are around you, waiting to be grasped and utilized. This book gives you the means to put Magick into your life, shows you how to make and use the tools, and gives you spells for every purpose

0-87542-121-0, 176 pgs., 5¼ x 8, illus., softcover $9.95

EARTH, AIR, FIRE & WATER
More Techniques of Natural Magic
by Scott Cunningham

A water-smoothed stone . . . The wind . . . A candle's flame . . . A pool of water. These are the age-old tools of natural magic. Born of the Earth, possessing inner power, they await only our touch and intention to bring them to life.

The four Elements are the ancient powerhouses of magic. Using their energies, we can transform ourselves, our lives and our worlds. Tap into the marvelous powers of the natural world with these rites, spells and simple rituals that you can do easily and with a minimum of equipment. *Earth, Air, Fire & Water* includes more than 75 spells, rituals and ceremonies; detailed instructions for designing your own magical spells; instills a sense of wonder concerning our planet and our lives; and promotes a natural, positive practice that anyone can successfully perform.

0-897542-131-8, 240 pgs., 6 x 9, illus., softcover $9.95

Prices subject to change without notice.

THE TRUTH ABOUT WITCHCRAFT TODAY
by Scott Cunningham

Here is the first real look at the facts about Witchcraft and the religion of Wicca. For centuries, organized religions have perpetrated lies about the ancient practice of Witchcraft, and to this day many misinformed people think Wicca involves worship of the Devil, sex orgies, and drug use. It just isn't so! As Cunningham plainly states, the practice of magic is not supernatural or Satanic. Witches and folk magicians are only utilizing, through timeless rituals, natural energies found within the Earth and our bodies to enrich life by creating positive change.

If you are completely unfamiliar with Witchcraft, and have wondered exactly how magic works, this book was written for you! In a straightforward, easy-to-understand manner, Cunningham explains the differences between folk magic, ritual magic, ceremonial magic, and religious magic. He describes the folk magician's "tools of power" crystals, herbs, candles, and chants—as well as the ritual tools of the Wiccan: the athame, cauldron, crystal sphere and pentacle, among others. He also provides an excellent introduction to the practice of magic by delineating two simple folk magic spells, a circle-casting ceremony, and complete Wiccan ritual.

0-87542-127-X, 208 pgs., mass market $4.99

TO RIDE A SILVER BROOMSTICK
New Generation Witchcraft
by Silver RavenWolf

Throughout the world there is a new generation of Witches —people practicing or wishing to practice the craft on their own, without an in-the-flesh magickal support group. *To Ride a Silver Broomstick* speaks to those people, presenting them with both the science and religion of Witchcraft, allowing them to become active participants while growing at their own pace. It is ideal for anyone: male or female, young or old, those familiar with Witchcraft, and those totally new to the subject and unsure of how to get started.

Full of the author's warmth, humor and personal anecdotes, *To Ride a Silver Broomstick* leads you step-by-step through the various lessons with exercises and journal writing assignments. This is the complete Witchcraft 101, teaching you to celebrate the Sabbats, deal with coming out of the broom closet, choose a magickal name, visualize the Goddess and God, meditate, design a sacred space, acquire magickal tools, design and perform rituals, network, spell cast, perform color and candle magick, divination, healing, telepathy, psychometry, astral projection, and much, much more.

0-87542-791-X, 320 pgs., 7 x 10, illus., softcover $14.95

WITCHCRAFT TODAY, BOOK ONE
The Modern Craft Movement
edited by Chas S. Clifton

For those already in the Craft, and for those who stand outside the ritual circle wondering if it is the place for them, *Witchcraft Today 1* brings together the writings of nine well-known Neopagans who give a cross-section of the beliefs and practices of this diverse and fascinating religion.

The contributors live in cities, small towns and rural areas, from California to Ireland, and they have all claimed a magical birthright—that lies open to any committed person—of healing, divination, counseling and working with the world's cycles.

Written specifically for this volume, the articles include:
- "A Quick History of Witchcraft's Revival" by Chas S. Clifton
- "An Insider's Look at Pagan Festivals" by Oz
- "Seasonal Rites and Magical Rites" by Pauline Campanelli
- "Witchcraft and Healing" by Morwyn
- "Sex Magic" by Valerie Voigt
- "Men and Women in Witchcraft" by Janet and Stewart Farrar
- "Witches and the Earth" by Chas S. Clifton
- "The Solo Witch" by Heather O'Dell
- "Witchcraft and the Law" by Pete Pathfinder Davis
- "Witchcraft and Shamanism" by Grey Cat
- "Being a Pagan in a 9-to-5 World" by Valerie Voigt

Also included are additional resources for Wiccans including publications, mail order suppliers, pagan organizations, computer bulletin boards and special-interest resources. The Principles of Wiccan Belief are also restated here.

0-87542-377-9, 208 pgs., 5¼ x 8, softcover $9.95

WITCHCRAFT TODAY, BOOK TWO
Rites of Passage
edited by Chas S. Clifton

This book is about the ritual glue that binds Pagan culture. In contrast, much writing on modern Paganism, whether it be Witchcraft or some other form, seems to assume that the reader is a young, single adult—a "seeker." At most, the reader is seen as a member of a coven or other group made up of adults. This collection of writings, however, takes a wider view with the long-term goal of presenting a living Pagan culture. If modern Pagan traditions are to persist and have any effect on the world community in an overt way, they must encompass people of all ages, not just young adults. *Witchcraft Today, Book Two: Rites of Passage*, therefore, is organized according to some of life's significant markers: birth, puberty, adulthood, partnership, parenthood, Wicca conversion, maturity or eldership, and finally death. None of these occur in a social vacuum, but always in relation to other people.

- Childbirth and Wiccaning—Patricia Telesco
- Raising a Pagan Child—Karen Charboneau-Harrison
- Between the Worlds: Late Adolescence and Early Adulthood in Modern Paganism—Anodea Judith
- Working with the Underaged Seeker—Judy Harrow
- Reflections on Conversion to Wicca—by Darcie
- Initiation by Ordeal: Military Service as a Passage into Adulthood—by Judy Harrow
- Handfasting: Marriage and the Modern Pagan— by Jeff Charboneau-Harrison
- Puberty Rites for Adult Women—by Oz
- Pagan Approaches to Illness, Grief and Loss— by Paul Suliin
- Witches after 40—by Grey Cat
- Pagan Rites of Dying—by Oz

0-87542-378-7, 288 pgs., 5¼ x 8, softcover $9.95

WITCHCRAFT TODAY: BOOK THREE
Witchcraft & Shamanism
edited by Chas S. Clifton

This book is a compelling and honest examination of shamanic techniques (both classical and neo-) as they are being practiced in Neopagan Witchcraft in the 1990s. Shamanism is a natural adjunct to the ritualistic and magical practice of many covens and solitary Pagans. In this ground-breaking volume, you will discover how others have integrated techniques such as trance journeys, soul retrieval, and altered states of consciousness.

Discover how shamanic ideas influenced Greek philosophers, Platonists, Pythagoreans and Gnostics ... learn how evidence from the old witch trials suggests that at least some Europeans may have practiced shamanic journeying in the past ... incorporate caves for ritual and inner journeys, both literally and in visualization ... find out who is out there retrieving souls and curing elfshot ... compare the guided visualizations common to modern magickal practice with the neo-shamanic journey ... learn how spirit contacts are made, how guides are perceived and what "worlds" they reside in ... and much more.

ISBN: 1-56718-150-3, 288 pgs., 5¼ x 8, photos, softcover $9.95

CIRCLE OF THE COSMIC MUSE
by Maria Kay Simms

Circle of the Cosmic Muse integrates Wiccan ritual practice and astrological knowledge. It contains complete rituals—based closely on astrological symbolism—for one full year of Esbats and Sabbats, plus rituals for special occasions such as weddings, funerals, blessing and naming children. For astrologers who seek to bring the energy of planetary cycles into a personal experience, the rituals are beautifully constructed and easy to follow. For the Wiccan looking to blend ritual practice into the "cosmic" scheme of things, the astrological information is presented in an easy-to-understand and direct fashion.

Additionally, this book is a detailed "how-to" for setting up and running a Wiccan circle, and it offers a unique perspective on the philosophy and ethical framework of Wiccan practice. There are many paths to truth, many ways to seek the Goddess and God within. With this book, you have an example of one path, one system, that you can use in part or as a whole, just as you choose.

1-56718-656-4, 496 pgs., 6 x 9, illus., softcover $17.95

THE LLEWELLYN ANNUALS

Llewellyn's MOON SIGN BOOK: Approximately 500 pages of valuable information on gardening, fishing, weather, stock market forecasts, personal horoscopes, good planting dates, and general instructions for finding the best date to do just about anything! Articles by prominent forecasters and writers in the fields of gardening, astrology, politics, economics and cycles. This special almanac, different from any other, has been published annually since 1906. It's fun, informative and has been a great help to millions in their daily planning. **State year $4.99**

Llewellyn's SUN SIGN BOOK: Your personal horoscope for the entire year! All 12 signs are included in one handy book. Also included are forecasts, special feature articles, and an action guide for each sign. Monthly horoscopes are written by Gloria Star, author of *Optimum Child*, for your personal sun sign and there are articles on a variety of subjects written by well-known astrologers from around the country. Much more than just a horoscope guide! Entertaining and fun the year around. **State year $4.99**

Llewellyn's DAILY PLANETARY GUIDE: Includes all of the major daily aspects plus their exact times in Eastern and Pacific time zones, lunar phases, signs and voids plus their times, planetary motion, a monthly ephemeris, sunrise and sunset tables, special articles on the planets, signs, aspects, a business guide, planetary hours, rulerships, and much more. Large 5¼ x 8 format for more writing space, spiral bound to lie flat, address and phone listings, time-zone conversion chart and blank horoscope chart. **State year $7.95**

Llewellyn's ASTROLOGICAL CALENDAR: Large wall calendar of 48 pages. Beautiful full-color cover and full-color paintings inside. Includes special feature articles by famous astrologers, and complete introductory information on astrology. It also contains a lunar gardening guide, celestial phenomena, a blank horoscope chart, and monthly date pages which include aspects, Moon phases, signs and voids, planetary motion, an ephemeris, personal forecasts, lucky dates, planting and fishing dates, and more. 10 x 13 size. Set in Eastern time, with fold-down conversion table for other time zones worldwide. **State year $10.00**

Llewellyn's MAGICAL ALMANAC: This beautifully illustrated almanac explores traditional earth religions and folklore while focusing on magical myths. Each month is summarized in a two-page format with information that includes the phases of the moon, festivals and rites for the month, as well as detailed magical advice. This is an indispensable guide is for anyone who is interested in planning rituals, spells and other magical advice. It features writing by some of the most prominent authors in the field. **State year $6.95**

THE CRAFTED CUP
Ritual Mysteries of the Goddess and the Grail
by Shadwynn
The Holy Grail—fabled depository of wonder, enchantment and ultimate spiritual fulfillment—is the key by which the wellsprings of a Deeper Life can be tapped for the enhancement of our inner growth. *The Crafted Cup* is a compendium of the teachings and rituals of a distinctly Pagan religious Order—the *Ordo Arcanorum Gradalis*—which incorporates into its spiritual way of worship ritual imagery based upon the Arthurian Grail legends, a reverence towards the mythic Christ, and an appreciation of the core truths and techniques found scattered throughout the New Age movement.

The Crafted Cup is divided into two parts. The first deals specifically with the teachings and general concepts which hold a central place within the philosophy of the *Ordo Arcanorum Gradalis*. The second and larger of the two parts is a complete compilation of the sacramental rites and seasonal rituals which make up the liturgical calendar of the Order. It contains one of the largest collections of Pagan, Grail-oriented rituals yet published.
0-87542-739-1, 420 pgs., 7 x 10, illus., softcover $19.95

THE FAMILY WICCA BOOK
The Craft for Parents & Children
by Ashleen O'Gaea
Enjoy the first book written for Pagan parents! The number of Witches raising children to the Craft is growing. The need for mutual support is rising—yet until now, there have been no books that speak to a Wiccan family's needs and experience. Finally, here is *The Family Wicca Book*, full to the brim with rituals, projects, encouragement and practical discussion of real-life challenges. You'll find lots of ideas to use right away.

Is magic safe for children? Why do some people think Wiccans are Satanists? How do you make friends with spirits and little people in the local woods? Find out how one Wiccan family gives clear and honest answers to questions that intrigue pagans all over the world.

When you want to ground your family in Wicca without ugly "bashing;" explain life, sex, and death without embarrassment; and add to your Sabbats without much trouble or expense, *The Family Wicca Book* is required reading. You'll refer to it again and again as your traditions grow with your family.
0-87542-591-7, 240 pgs., 5¼ x 8, illus., softcover $9.95

Prices subject to change without notice.

THE PAGAN FAMILY
Handing Down the Old Ways
by Ceisiwr Serith

Neo-Paganism is growing fast. Not only is it growing in numbers, but its members are growing up. They are starting families, and they have discovered that they are pretty much on their own when it comes to blending their alternative spirituality with child-rearing. Rituals and training exercises that work well with adults often do not work with children. *The Pagan Family* will be a welcome guide in the home of all Pagan parents, saving them time, research and trial and error.

Pagans who wish to celebrate their religion as a family will find general advice on the construction of rituals—as well as ritual guidelines for weddings, births, birthdays, seasonal celebrations, lunar phases, coming of age, divorce, and death. *The Pagan Family* provides suggestions for the creation of the sacred home (including blessings and household shrines) ... activities for children such as meditations, mask and rattle making, drumming, storytelling ... suggested prayers for throughout the day ... and provides many tips for teaching children about Paganism. References and resources for further information are included in the appendices.

0-87542-210-1, 310 pgs., 6 x 9, softcover $12.95

THE SABBATS
A New Approach to Living the Old Ways
Edain McCoy

The Sabbats offers many fresh, exciting ways to deepen your connection to the turning of the Wheel of the Year. This tremendously practical guide to Pagan solar festivals does more than teach you about the "old ways"—you will learn workable ideas for combining old customs with new expressions of those beliefs that will be congruent with your lifestyle and tradition.

The Sabbats begins with background on Paganism (tenets, teachings, and tools) and origins of the eight Sabbats, followed by comprehensive chapters on each Sabbat. These pages are full of ideas for inexpensive seasonal parties in which Pagans and non-Pagans alike can participate, as well as numerous craft ideas and recipes to enrich your celebrations. The last section provides 16 complete texts of Sabbat rituals—for both covens and solitaries—with detailed guidelines for adapting rituals to specific traditions or individual tastes. Includes an extensive reference section with a resources guide, bibliography, musical scores for rituals, and more.

This book may contain the most practical advice ever for incorporating the old ways into your Pagan lifestyle!

1-56718-663-7, 7 x 10, 320 pp., illus., photos, softcover $14.95

Prices subject to change without notice.